Whimsical Wishes
And Other Storybook Themes

by Maxine Riggers
illustrated by Marilynn G. Barr
cover art by Terrence Meagher

Publisher: Roberta Suid
Copy Editor: Carol Whiteley
Design and Production: Susan Pinkerton

Maxine Riggers is a former kindergarten teacher who has been telling stories at libraries and schools for over 12 years. She is the author of Amazing Alligators and other Story Hour Friends, and has instructed librarians on how to hold successful story hours.

Unless otherwise noted, Maxine Riggers is the author of all poems, songs, and finger plays.

Monday Morning is a registered trademark of
Monday Morning Books, Inc.

ISBN 1-878279-64-5

Printed in the United States of America
9 8 7 6 5 4 3 2 1

CONTENTS

Storytellers, teachers, librarians, parents—this book is meant for you. Its six chapters are filled with ideas for enhancing children's interest in literature. Each chapter focuses on a specific theme and provides information on several carefully selected picture books that relate to that theme. WHIMSICAL WISHES covers circuses, dreams, folk and fairy tales, magic, make-believe, and (of course) wishes. The chapters offer exciting and enriching theme-related activities including read-aloud ideas, poems, songs, finger plays and action verses, crafts, games, dramatic play, and cooking suggestions. A "More Stories" section in each chapter contains a synopsis of additional lap books and read-alouds.

Award-Winning Books

Each year, the Caldecott Medal is awarded for the most distinguished illustrations in an American picture book. Caldecott Honor Books are also chosen. A copy of the award seal appears on the cover of the books receiving this honor. As you read medal award winners with the children, discuss the seal and what it means. The children will learn to associate the award with good books. The Coretta Scott King Medal is also awarded yearly to an excellent African-American book, and a copy of this seal appears on the covers of these books. Be sure to discuss this medal and its meaning with the children.

To find out which books have received the Caldecott Medal, refer to THE CALDECOTT AWARD: THE WINNERS AND THE HONOR BOOKS by Bertha Woolman and Patricia Utsey. A "Children's Choices" annual list is also available, published each year by the International Reading Association-Children's Book Council Joint Committee.

Big Books

Big Book versions of children's books are gaining in popularity for many reasons: their size is appealing to children and adults alike, readers enjoy the colorful illustrations, and the large print and illustrations allow a group of children to easily see and share the story together. If you haven't worked with them before, give them a try. It's best to place Big Books on an easel while reading. The pages lie flat and can be seen by all the children. For a catalog of Big Books: Scholastic, Inc., P.O. Box 7602, Jefferson City, MO 65102.

Dramatic Play

Dramatic play encourages creativity, cooperation, problem solving, and the development of oral expression. While acting out a story, children restate what they hear in their own words. They use facial expressions to create different moods: sad, happy, or angry. They use different vocal expressions to fit the various characters.

To encourage learning and self-expression, set up a center for dramatic play. Suggestions are made in the "Setting the Stage" section of each chapter. Be sure to change the center frequently, and always include a mirror for children to incorporate. (Is it a magic mirror, like the one in THROUGH THE LOOKING GLASS?) Sometimes it only takes one little prop to get children motivated to dramatize a favorite story. And with encouragement and support, thet may soon be creating their own stories!

Let's go to the circus! After reading a few circus books (consider donning a clown suit while reading), the children will undoubtedly want to hold their very own big tent extravaganza. They will delight in making all of the necessary preparations and performing the circus acts for an audience of their peers. Clown suits may be purchased or rented from costume shops or sewn (check pattern books). Simple costumes can also be made from a paper hat, mask, or a silly rubber nose. Anything out of the ordinary will put children in a fanciful mood.

Invite a professional clown to visit the classroom to talk with the children and to perform. Check to see if a circus or rodeo is coming to town and if clowns are available and willing to advertise their show. The ultimate field trip for this theme would be to visit a circus in action.

SETTING THE STAGE

Ask the children to help decorate the room with colorful banners, balloons, and pictures of clowns and circus animals. Create circus animals by dressing stuffed toys in circus attire: put a colorful blanket and head piece on an elephant or a camel, a clown hat on a dog, a vest and hat on a monkey, and a ruffled skirt on a bear. Place plenty of circus books near the animals, and position a few animals as if they're reading from one of the books. Title this display "The Circus Is in Town."

Make a big top tent from poster paper, then color, cut out, and glue it to the front of a box. Place circus books inside the box, and invite children to read them.

Dress a stuffed bear similar to Little Bear in LITTLE BEAR AND THE PAPAGINI CIRCUS by Margaret Greaves and display it beside the book. Set a clown in the reading corner with a sign around its neck that says, "Please read to me."

Create a flannel board circus by collecting or making the different circus elements: tents, cages, ringmaster, animals, tickets, food, and more. Glue flannel to the back of each drawing or object and make all of them readily available for the children to use when creating their own circuses.

BULLETIN BOARD IDEAS

1. Enlarge the "Clown Around with Books" illustration and color the picture. Make the clown three-dimensional by adding yarn for hair, tassels for his hat and suit, a fuzzy ball for his nose, and a real tie.

2. Title a bulletin board "Encore for Eleanor." After reading this book, ask the children to draw Eleanor. Pin up their drawings. Children love to see their own artwork on display. GINGER JUMPS would be another good book for this activity.

3. Make animal cages for a "Circus Animal" display. Cut several sheets of colored construction paper into rectangles the size of drinking straws. Staple straws at the top and bottom to resemble cage bars. Label the various cages with names of different animals. Ask the children to draw their favorite circus animal and insert them behind the bars.

Clown Around With BOOKS

GINGER JUMPS

THUMB PRINT CIRCUS

I WANT TO GO TO THE CIRCUS

DUMBO

THE CIRCUS

CLIFFORD AT THE CIRCUS

CHESTER THE WORLDLY PIG
by Bill Peet (Houghton Mifflin, 1965).

Story: Chester, a spotted pig, has his heart set on becoming a star performer in the circus. He practices his special trick, but doesn't get a job, and returns to the farm to live the life of an ordinary pig. One day, a carnival man discovers that Chester's spots are in the shape of a world map, and the little pig becomes the "Worldly Pig."

Materials: Chester, performing platform

Directions: Make a big Chester pig from pink poster paper. Draw the map on both sides of the pig. Stand him on a platform on his nose by sliding his nose through a slit in it. Introduce the pig to the children, and explain that the spotted pig's name is Chester and that he wants to join the circus. At the end of the story, let the children discover how his spots are in the shape of the world. Refer to Circus Crafts for directions on making a Chester puppet.

CLARA JOINS THE CIRCUS
by Michael Pellowski, il. by True Kelley (Parents Magazine Press, 1981).

Story: Clara Cow is bored with her way of life and goes to town to join the circus. She is hopelessly unsuitable for tightrope walking, juggling, hanging from a trapeze, and being shot from a cannon. Finally, she finds a job with the clowns that is perfect for her.

Materials: juggling balls, beanbags, rope, peanuts, popcorn, tape, tumbling mats, umbrella

Directions: After reading the story, provide soft juggling balls or beanbags (two at first) for juggling practice. Tape a rope to the floor for balancing on the "high wire." Provide a small umbrella for the high wire rope walking. Place mats on the floor for tumblers. Ask the children to brainstorm other acts they might like to try. Hold a circus with the children performing their various acts. Serve peanuts and popcorn.

GINGER JUMPS
by Lisa Campbell Ernst (Bradbury, 1990).

Story: Ginger, a small brown dog, has grown up in the circus, but she dreams of belonging to a family. She searches the crowd during each performance for the little girl in her dreams. In the search, Ginger is pestered by an applause-happy poodle, Prunella. When Prunella twists her toe and can't jump from the platform, Ginger jumps in her place and lands right in the arms of the little girl in her dreams.

Materials: Jumping Ginger poster, stuffed toy or puppet dog

Directions: Beforehand, dress a stuffed dog with a neck ruffle to resemble Ginger. Reproduce the "Now Appearing! Jumping Ginger" poster as it appears in the book. Show the poster to the children and let them speculate what the story might be. Later, pin the poster on the wall as a fond memory of the loving circus dog, Ginger. After reading the story, introduce Ginger. With the help of the children, reenact Ginger's adventures at the circus.

LOUELLA AND THE YELLOW BALLOON
by Molly Coxe (Crowell, 1988).

Story: Patricia Pig takes Louella, her baby pig, to the circus. The best circus act of the day begins when Louella loses her yellow balloon and chases it through the circus. She passes a bicycling bear, a fierce lion, and a balancing mouse. Patricia and Louella are united again on the tightrope as the crowd cheers.

Materials: yellow helium-filled balloon, yellow balloon shapes cut from construction paper

Directions: Hold the balloon and explain that it is filled with helium. Ask the children what they think will happen if you let go of the string. Before reading the story, let the balloon go and watch it float about the room. Give each child a yellow construction paper balloon. Let the children take their paper balloons home to use as a prop when telling the story to someone else.

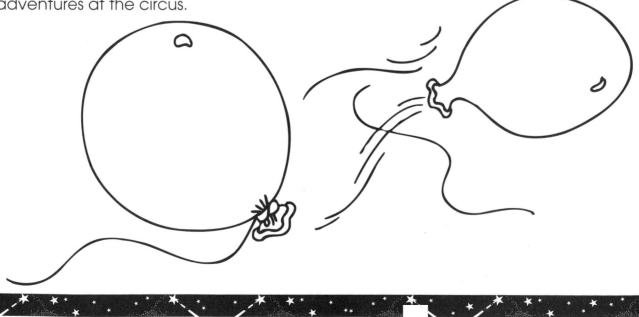

THE MAN ON THE FLYING TRAPEZE

by Robert Quackenbush (Lippincott, 1975).

Story: This popular book tells about the life of Emmett Kelly Sr., a famous clown. Emmett Kelly Sr. was a man on the flying trapeze until the Great Depression. Then he was forced to take a job as a hobo circus clown. The verse is set to music, "The Man on the Flying Trapeze," which is included in the book.

Materials: hobo clothes

Directions: Before reading this story, dress up like a hobo clown. Wear big pants with patches, old shoes, a colorful bandanna, and a tattered hat. Teach "The Man on the Flying Trapeze" song to the children and sing it several times. Provide dress-up hobo clothes for the children to wear during dramatic play, and encourage them to clown around.

THUMBPRINT CIRCUS

by Rodney Peppe (Delacorte, 1988).

Story: Thumbkin, a little clown made from a thumbprint, wants to join the circus. Thumbkin helps all the thumbprint circus animals—the bears, elephants, chimps, seals, and tigers. When Thumbkin takes a ride as a human cannonball, he becomes the star of the show.

Materials: ink pad, drawing paper, crayons or markers

Directions: After reading the story, let the children try their hand at thumbprint art. Provide an ink pad for children to make thumbprints on drawing paper. They can complete their circus characters with crayons or markers. Display the art on the bulletin board under the heading "Our Thumbprint Circus." Another circus book by this author is CIRCUS NUMBERS.

Blos, Joan W., il. by Irene Trivas. **LOTTIE'S CIRCUS** (Morrow, 1989).

In Lottie's imagination, she and her cat, Famous, conjure up a wonderful circus. She performs a dazzling high-wire act and magic tricks. She's a clown, the ticket seller, and the World's Tallest Lady. When the show is over, Lottie makes plans for an even better circus next time.

Bond, Michael and Fred Banbery. **PADDINGTON AT THE CIRCUS** (Random House, 1973).

Paddington Bear accidentally gets involved in the trapeze act at the circus. A clown rescues Paddington from the swing, and Paddington becomes the star of the circus. In reality, however, he enjoys the safety of his own bed later that night.

Bridwell, Norman. **CLIFFORD AT THE CIRCUS** (Scholastic, 1977).

Emily Elizabeth and her big dog Clifford answer the "Help Wanted" sign at the circus. The fun begins when Clifford walks the tightrope, becomes a clown, disguises himself as an elephant, catches the high diver on his tongue, and performs the most exciting end to a circus ever!

Brunhoff, Laurent de. **BABAR'S LITTLE CIRCUS STAR** (Random House, 1988).

In this story about the famous elephant Babar, Isabelle is very disappointed about being the smallest elephant in the family. When she's given a chance to perform in the circus, all ends well.

Cole, Joanna, il. by Jerry Smath. **THE CLOWN-AROUNDS GO ON VACATION** (Parents Magazine Press, 1983).

The Clown-Around family is on their way to visit Uncle Waldo. Along the way they have many hilarious misadventures. They find a "fork" in the road and a "fast-food" restaurant where the food runs about! Other books about the Clown-Around family include THE CLOWN-AROUNDS, THE CLOWN-AROUNDS HAVE A PARTY, and GET WELL, CLOWN-AROUNDS.

Daugherty, James. **ANDY AND THE LION** (Viking, 1966).

Andy reads a book about lions and, as a result, there are lions in his dreams. Andy even believes that he finds a real lion on his way to school. The two become friends, but each must go his own way. When the circus comes to town they are happily reunited.

De Paola, Tomie. **JINGLE, THE CHRISTMAS CLOWN** (Putnam, 1992).

The circus will not hold its usual Christmas Eve performance in a little Italian village because the "old timers" have left the circus. Luckily, Jingle, the clown, stays behind to care for the animals, and together they offer a very special performance.

De Regniers, Beatrice Schenk. **CIRCUS** (Viking, 1966).

This rhyming book of photos depicts the circus from beginning to end. It shows clowns, tightrope walkers, bears, elephants, horses, lions, acrobats, stunt people, circus food, and finally the parade of performers.

Disney, Walt. **DUMBO** (Western, 1977).

Dumbo doesn't like having over-sized ears because he's always being teased. Then he learns to use his big ears to fly and becomes the star performer.

Du Bois, William Pene. **BEAR CIRCUS** (Viking, 1971).

The Koala Park bears must leave their home because grasshoppers have eaten all the gum tree leaves. As the bears are moving, they meet some friendly kangaroos who offer them a ride in their pouches. To show their appreciation, the bears perform circus acts for the kangaroos' enjoyment.

Ehlert, Lois. **CIRCUS** (HarperCollins, 1992).

The ringmaster directs the audience to watch the array of performers. In this circus, readers will witness The Pretzel Brothers, Hugo the World's Biggest Elephant, Samu the Tiger, marching snakes, leaping lizards, the lion and his trainer, and the lovable clowns.

Falwell, Cathryn. **CLOWNING AROUND** (Orchard, 1991).

An ingenious clown magically creates a car, a dog jumping through a hoop, a dancing doll, and a colorful ball. He "clowns around" with letters to spell a variety of words that will be easy for very young children to read.

Fox, Charles Philip. **COME TO THE CIRCUS** (Reilly and Lee, 1960).

Barbara and Peter go to the circus with special wishes. Peter wants to pet the big circus snake, and Barbara hopes she can ride a white circus horse. They see the animals, clowns, and all the entertaining performances, and their wishes do come true.

Goennel, Heidi. **THE CIRCUS** (Tambourine, 1992).

A group of young children watch as a circus troop comes to town to set up the tightrope, the trapeze, and the circus rings. They get to see the performers practice, and they are thrilled to watch the actual big show performance.

Greaves, Margaret, il. by Francesca Crespi. **LITTLE BEAR AND THE PAPAGINI CIRCUS** (Dial, 1986).

Little Bear longs to participate in the circus just like his father, mother, big brother, and little sister, but everyone says that his job is to stay out of the way. On opening night, Little Bear accidentally slips into the center ring and becomes the star of the show.

Harmer, Mabel. **THE CIRCUS** (Regensteiner, 1981).

The circus moves to town and sets up the tents. The lions, tigers, leopards, horses, and elephants all have their special cages. Tightrope wires are strung and seats are set up for the audience. At last, it's time for the show to begin!

Harrls, Steven Michael, il. by Norma Welliver. **THIS IS MY TRUNK** (Atheneum, 1985).

A clown's trunk is his closet, workshop, dresser, and office. In this book, a clown prepares for his performance. He puts on his special clothes, a funny hat, and uses makeup to create his clown face. When it's time for the show, he performs stunts, tricks, and gags to make the audience (and readers) laugh.

Hol, Coby. **HENRIETTA SAVES THE SHOW** (North-South, 1991).

A little white pony named Henrietta loves the farm where she lives. She enjoys galloping across the fields and pulling the farmer's milk wagon. But one day, the circus comes to town and Henrietta gets to fill in for a sick horse in the most important act in the circus.

Huber, Ursula, il. by Celestino Piatti. **THE NOCK FAMILY CIRCUS** (Atheneum, 1968).

This book relates the true events of the famous Nock Family Circus. The caravan stops in a field and erects a big tent. Each performer prepares for his or her act. Aunt Veronica cooks for everyone and Grandpa Nock is the ringmaster. When the performance ends, the family packs up and drives over the dusty country roads to another town.

Jacobs, Allen D. and Leland B., il. by Hans Baltzer. **BEHIND THE CIRCUS TENT** (Lerner, 1967).

The animals behind the circus tent prepare for their performances. The seals balance balls, the bears rest, a horse dances to music, and the monkeys play hide and seek.

Keremes, Constance Andrea, il. by Toni Goffe. **I WANTED TO GO TO THE CIRCUS** (Harbinger House, 1989).

A young boy's parents force him to attend the ballet when he would much rather go to the circus. At first, the boy is quite bored with the ballet. Then an evil magician performs, and the boy shouts with glee. The audience joins in on his exuberance. However, even though the boy enjoys the performance, he still wishes popcorn was sold at the theater.

Knight, Hilary. **THE CIRCUS IS COMING** (Golden Press, 1978).

A parade of circus entertainers wanders down the street inviting all the children to come to the circus. "Come one, come all!" shouts the clown. He is followed by musicians, animals, acrobats, and the human cannonball.

Kraus, Robert. **HOW SPIDER SAVED THE FLEA CIRCUS** (Scholastic, 1991).

Spider works hard at the circus to earn tickets for his friends, Ladybug and Fly. When Spider earns only one ticket, the three friends manage to outsmart the ticket man. When all of the flea performers leave, Spider and his friends step in to save the show.

McCully, Emily. **MIRETTE ON THE HIGH WIRE** (Putnam, 1992).

In this circus tale, Mirette is attracted to Bellini, a high wire performer visiting her mother's boarding house. Mirette learns to walk the high wire and helps Bellini regain his confidence so he can perform again. The two set off on a new career together.

Maestro, Betsy and Giulio. **HARRIET GOES TO THE CIRCUS** (Crown, 1977).

In this number concept book, Harriet the elephant is determined to be first in line at the circus. Her friends line up behind her, but, when the circus tent opens, the tenth friend turns out to be first in line. Luckily, the seats are in a circle and no one is first or last!

Moers, Hermann, il. by Jozef Wilkon. **TONIO THE GREAT** (North-South, 1990).

Tonio is the finest acrobat in the circus and is famous for his performance on the high wire and his unicycle act. However, when Tonio sees a sparrow fall, he loses his nerve.

Ostheeren, Ingrid, il. by Agnes Mathieu. **JONATHAN MOUSE AT THE CIRCUS** (North-South, 1988).

Jonathan Mouse gets into trouble when the circus comes to town. He wants to help, but accidentally lets the star monkey out of his cage. Happily, Jonathan finds the monkey and saves the show.

Peet, Bill. **ENCORE FOR ELEANOR** (Houghton Mifflin, 1981).

Eleanor the elephant is a star performer in the circus. She's the only one who can walk on a pair of stilts. However, after 40 years she becomes too old to perform and is sent off to the zoo. Eleanor finds happiness again when she begins drawing pictures with her trunk.

Peet, Bill. **PAMELA CAMEL** (Houghton Mifflin, 1984).

Pamela Camel, a dejected circus camel, prevents a train from wrecking on a broken rail. Pamela then becomes a star attraction at the circus.

Peet, Bill. **RANDY'S DANDY LIONS** (Houghton Mifflin, 1964).

The circus is wonderful except for the lion act. Randy, the lion tamer, has trained his lions well, but they're too shy to perform for a crowd. After some miserable performances, the lions finally overcome stage fright and learn to love the spotlight.

Petersham, Maud and Miska. **THE CIRCUS BABY** (Macmillan, 1989).

Mother Elephant decides that her baby should learn to eat properly, just like the baby in the clown family. Unfortunately, the baby elephant doesn't fit in the highchair and finds it most difficult to eat with a spoon. A total disaster develops, and Mother Elephant learns an important lesson—it's best for her baby to be herself.

Piumini, Roberto, il. by Barry Root. **THE SAINT AND THE CIRCUS** (Tambourine, 1991).

There's trouble at the Bumbellini Circus when Filofilo, the acrobat, can't keep his balance. If he doesn't get help quick, he will plummet a hundred feet without a safety net. He says a prayer and the bumbling Saint Tony sends a whole menagerie of creatures to help.

Poult, Virginia, il. by Mary Maloney-Fleming. **BLUE BUG'S CIRCUS** (Children's Press, 1977).

Blue Bug unsuccessfully attempts a variety of circus acts. He tries to roll a ball, lift weights, sing, and tumble. It's not until he becomes a clown that Blue Bug finds success.

CIRCUS CLOWN

I love the funny clown,
A rainbow in his many colors
As he dances all around.
His big, round, bright red nose
Is a delight to see,
As are his oversized toes.
Oh, what fun it must be
To be a circus clown
Who loves to entertain me!

THREE LITTLE MONKEYS

I know something I won't tell—
Three little monkeys in a peanut shell!
One can sing and one can dance,
And one can make a pair of pants.
—Anonymous

SAMMY THE CLOWN

Sammy the Clown jumps all around.
(Jump in different directions.)
He juggles balls till they fall down.
(Pretend to juggle and let the balls fall
  down.)
And his round, red nose
Makes me laugh and shout.
(Laugh and shout, "Hooray!")

CLOWNS

Clowns have great big feet,
(Kick feet.)
And smile at everyone they meet.
(Smile.)
Clowns jump in the air,
(Jump with arms up.)
And down again, if they dare.
Clowns have a funny face,
(Make a face.)
And ears that flap in place.
(Put hands behind ears.)
At the end of the show,
The clowns sit down just so!
(Sit with legs crossed.)

More Circus Poems

"Clooney the Clown," p. 31 in A LIGHT IN THE ATTIC by Shel Silverstein (Harper & Row, 1981).

"The Acrobats," p. 10 and "It's Dark in Here," p. 21 in WHERE THE SIDEWALK ENDS by Shel Silverstein (Harper & Row, 1974).

Circus Poem Book

CIRCUS! CIRCUS! poems selected by Lee Bennett Hopkins, il. by John O'Brien (Knopf, 1982).

More Action Verses and Finger Plays

"A Clown," p. 73 and "Don't Shake Hands with Tigers," p. 36 in MOVE OVER MOTHER GOOSE by Ruth I. Dowell, il. by Concetta C. Scott (Gryphon House, 1987).

"I'm a Little Puppet Clown," p. 48, "I Wish I Were a Circus Clown," p. 47, "This Little Clown," p. 92, and "Who Is It Mr. Clown?", p. 105 in RING A RING O'ROSES: FINGER PLAYS FOR PRESCHOOL CHILDREN (Flint Public Library, 1988).

 Circus Songs and Games

DOWN BY THE CIRCUS
(Tune: "Down by the Station")

Down by the circus early in the morning,
See the circus animals in their funny
  clothes.
See the funny clowns who jump and
  tumble over,
Hurry, hurry! Let's all go.

THE CIRCUS RING
(Tune: "The Mulberry Bush")
While singing the following song, suit
actions to words.

Here we go 'round the circus ring,
The circus ring, the circus ring.
Here we go 'round the circus ring,
So early in the morning.
This is the way we paint our face,
Paint our face, paint our face.
This is the way we paint our face,
So early in the morning.

Other verses: wear our hat, put on our
nose, stomp our feet, wear our wig

ELEPHANT TRAINER SAYS
(Play the same as "Simon Says.")

Elephant trainer says: stand on your hind
legs, stand on stool, bow to audience,
walk in circle, raise trunk, roll over. Ask for
other suggestions.

CIRCUS MIME

Hold a circus! Make advertising posters,
and tickets to give away to friends or
parents. Provide a box of clown clothes,
including big shoes, big pants with
patches, suspenders, neck ties, hats,
wigs, and big shirts for the children to
wear. Children can mime various acts,
such as juggling, balancing a ball like a
seal, riding a horse or elephant, flying
through the air (with the greatest of
ease) on a trapeze, balancing on a high
wire, taming a lion, or swinging from a
tree like a monkey.

TIGHTROPE WALKING

Provide an eight-foot, two-by-four board
to serve as the tightrope. Children take
turns walking the board. If they fall off,
they must return to the end of the line to
try again. Have a small umbrella handy
for them to use in this balancing act.

TRAINED LIONS

In this game, you need a Hula-Hoop, a
lion tamer, and some lions. The lion
tamer holds the Hula-Hoop on the
ground as the lions go through it.
Repeat, raising the Hula-Hoop a little
each time. If a child knocks down the
Hula-Hoop, the game starts over again
with the Hula-Hoop at ground level.

WORLDLY PIG PUPPET

Materials: pig pattern, Popsicle sticks, scissors, pink paper, crayons or colored markers, glue

Directions: Use the pattern to make two pink paper pigs for each child. Cut them out. Ask the children to draw a world map on the outside of each of their pigs. Give each child a Popsicle stick to glue to the insides of their pig patterns to make a two-sided pig. (It will be the same on both sides.) The children will want to make their worldly pig perform as Chester does in CHESTER THE WORLDLY PIG.

CLOWN HATS

Materials: newsprint, scissors, stapler, colored tissue or crepe paper, colored construction paper, glue

Directions: For each hat, fold a piece of newsprint in half. Cut on the dotted line as illustrated. Unfold. Roll into a cone shape and staple together to fit the child's head. Let the children decorate their hats with pompons made from newsprint or tissue paper and flowers cut from construction paper, or other decorations.

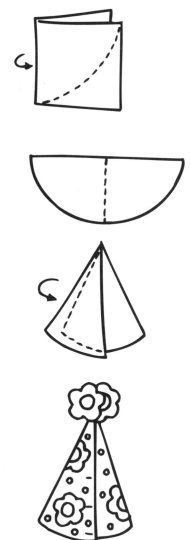

STAND-UP CIRCUS

Materials: tent and circus patterns, colored construction paper, scissors, crayons or colored markers

Directions: Let the children use the provided patterns to make a circus tent and various animals, or let them create some of their own. Have them cut out their creatures, color in features, and place in upright positions. Each child can make his or her own circus, or students can cooperate to make one big circus. Encourage the children to use the stand-up circus to create their own Big Top production.

CLOWN MASK

Materials: two clown patterns, stick, glue, scissors, colored markers

Directions: Copy and cut out the happy and sad clown patterns. Have the children decorate both masks with bright colors and cut out the eyes. Have the children glue a stick to the back side of one of the masks and then glue the two clown backs together. The children can change feelings very quickly by rotating the clown mask from one side to the other. Encourage the children to perform funny tricks while holding up the happy face and to tell sad stories with the sad face.

Tent Pattern

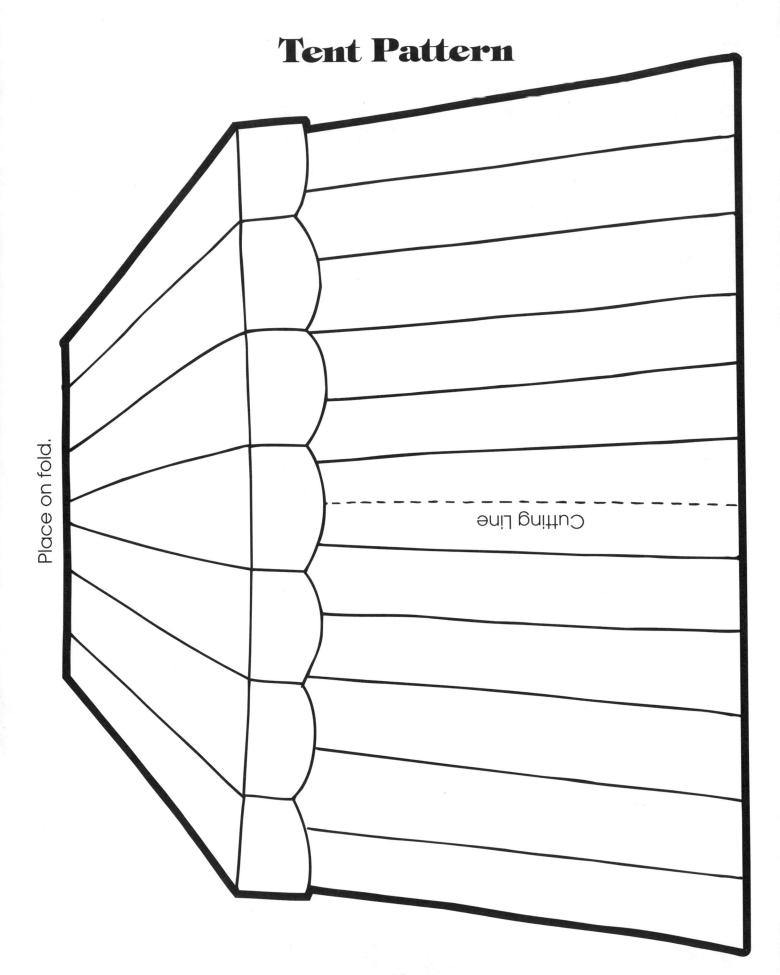

Place on fold.

Cutting Line

Circus Patterns

19

Clown Pattern

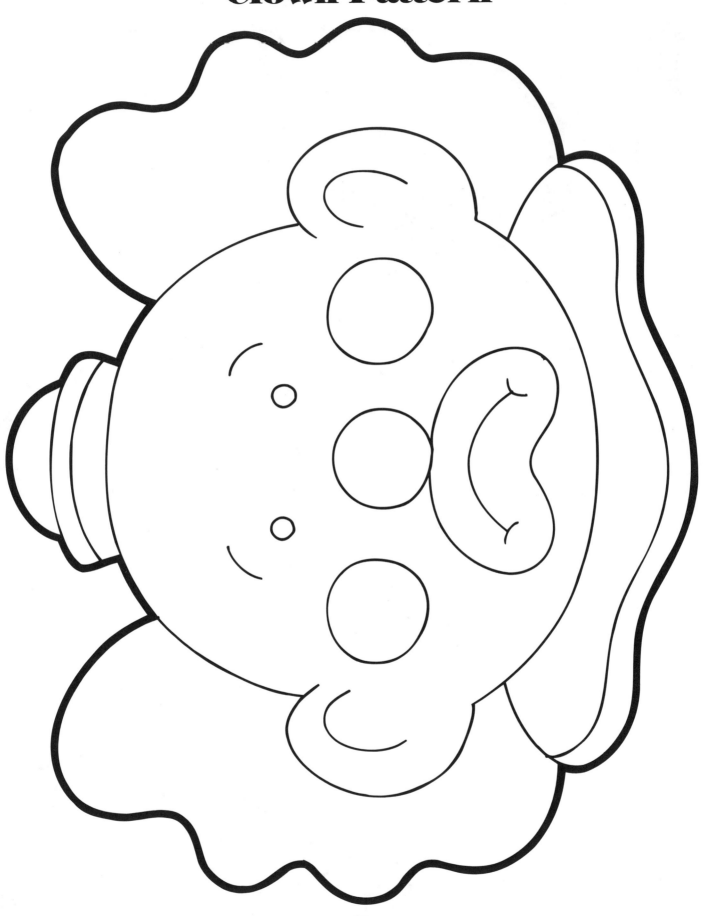

Clown Pattern

CIRCUS TREATS

Serve circus-type treats, such as sacks of popcorn, peanuts in the shell, hot dogs, soft pretzels, lemonade, snow cones, and cotton candy.

ANIMAL CRACKERS

Purchase boxes of animal crackers. Give one box to every two children. Encourage them to discuss the animals. Which ones might be found in a circus and what acts could they perform?

CLOWN ICE CREAM

For each child, place a rounded scoop of ice cream in a dish. Set a pointed ice cream cone on top of the scoop to form the clown's hat. Let children decorate the hat with colored candies stuck to the cone with frosting. Clown faces can be made on the ice cream with candies, sprinkles, and an assortment of cut fruit.

CUPCAKE CLOWN

Bake your favorite cupcakes in cupcake papers. Just before serving, place a scoop of ice cream on top of the cupcake. Let the children make faces and ears on the ice cream with candies or fruit. Place a large gumdrop on top for the clown's hat—you may want to use a toothpick to hold it on.

CIRCUS SANDWICHES

Let the children make their own peanut butter and jelly sandwiches. Provide animal cookie cutters to cut out the sandwiches in the shape of animals. Remind children not to throw away the scraps—they're good, too!!

LEMONADE

Make believe you're at the circus and set up a lemonade stand. The children will love taking turns at making the lemonade.

At bedtime, parents and children can be drawn close together by sharing stories. Stories that deal with dreams, night, and bedtime are both appropriate and fun for these special times.

On a designated day, ask the children to bring their pajamas to wear during story hour. Wear your night clothes at that time also. To create a dreamy atmosphere for reading in the classroom, turn off all the lights except for one small reading lamp. Provide children with blankets to cuddle in while listening to the stories.

Goodnight, sleep tight, don't let the bed bugs bite!

SETTING THE STAGE

Over the reading corner, hang stars and a big moon from the ceiling (see Dream Crafts). The children will delight in making these themselves. Also hang up the flying boat from THE DREAM CHILD (see Dream Crafts).

In the reading corner, provide pillows, blankets, teddy bears, large nightshirts, and recorded lullaby music for playing while reading.

Cover a cardboard box with black construction paper or spray paint. Glue or paint on stars and a moon. Store dream and bedtime books in this box, and encourage children to read them.

Make a bedroom in the house-keeping corner with beds, dolls, and stuffed animals. Provide books for the children to read to the dolls and stuffed animals.

Display a variety of night creatures such as owls, koalas, possums, and raccoons. Use stuffed animals or pictures.

BULLETIN BOARD IDEAS

1. Enlarge and copy the "Find a Dream in a Book" illustration. Color with pastel chalks and cut out. For a three-dimensional effect, use fluffy cotton or batting for the clouds. Glue book jackets or photocopies of book fronts onto the cotton. Cut out the titles and glue onto the clouds. Use a piece of fabric for the bed cover to complete the display.

2. Enlarge and copy some favorite characters from several of the books mentioned in this section, such as Benjamin Badger, Frances, and Owl. Color and cut out. Use an appropriate heading for each.

3. Title the board "When I'm Sleepy." Make a collage of various creatures and people sleeping, such as kittens curled up in a basket and bears sleeping in a cave. Older children will want to draw their own pictures for the collage.

4. Title the board "Moon Jumpers." Pin a full moon on a dark background along with a few trees. Ask the children to draw pictures of themselves to pin onto the background.

5. Make a collage of night workers, such as doctors, nurses, truck drivers, bakers, and police officers. Use pictures cut from old magazines or draw them.

THE DREAM CHILD
by David McPhail (Dutton, 1985).

Story: The Dream Child and Tame Bear climb into a boat with wings and sail into a night full of adventure. The two ask the frogs to hum softly so the chickens can roost. They also help a hungry lion and bring moonlight to the land of the giants.

Materials: teddy bears, flying boat (see Dream Crafts)

Directions: Give each child a teddy bear to hold while reading this story. Ask the children to imagine they're dream children holding their bears as they climb into a boat with wings. At the end of the story, have the children close their eyes and imagine they're falling asleep. Make a large flying boat and suspend it from the ceiling. The boat will remind the children about how wonderful dreams can be.

DREAMS
by Jack Keats (Macmillan, 1974).

Story: After Roberto makes a paper mouse at school, he wonders what it's capable of doing. He sets the mouse on the windowsill when he goes to sleep. During the night, when everyone else is asleep and dreaming, the paper mouse falls and its shadow rescues a cat by scaring away a barking dog.

Materials: paper mouse (see Dream Crafts), flashlight

Directions: Show the paper mouse to the children and ask them if they think this mouse can do anything. Can it talk? Can it walk? Set the mouse on a shelf and read the story. Later, experiment with the mouse and a flashlight to create a shadow as the mouse falls. The children will want to make their very own paper mouse to sit on their own bedroom windowsill.

GOODNIGHT MOON
by Margaret Wise Brown, il. by Clement Hurd (Harper, 1934).

Story: Before he goes to sleep, a little rabbit says goodnight to all of the familiar objects in his room: a toy house and a mouse, kittens and mittens, a comb and a brush, and finally to the noises of the night.

Materials: drawing materials, and an assortment of the following objects: telephone, red balloon, picture of a cow, picture of the three bears, two stuffed kittens, mittens, doll house, toy mouse, comb, brush, bowl of mush, stuffed rabbit, moon and stars in a window, clocks and socks

Directions: Place the objects listed above in the housekeeping center and encourage the children to recreate the room described in the story. They can draw and cut out pictures of any missing items. The children will have fun as they go up to each object and whisper goodnight before taking a nap. Or they may position the collected items in a box to make the bedroom.

GOOD NIGHT, OWL
by Pat Hutchins (Macmillan, 1972).

Story: Owl sits in his tree trying to sleep, but can't because the bees buzz, the crows creak, the starlings chatter, and the jays scream. But at night, all the tree inhabitants go to sleep, and it's Owl's turn to screech.

Materials: poster paper, markers or crayons, scissors, copy machine, flannel board

Directions: As you read this book, encourage the children to make animal sounds along with the characters in the story. Then ask various children to be the different creatures and have them all make the sounds simultaneously. For added interest, tell the story using a flannel board. Beforehand, draw a tree on poster paper, then color, cut out, and place on the flannel board. Use a copy machine to copy the book's tree inhabitants, then color, cut out, and add them to the branches of the tree as the story is told. Be sure to practice telling the story ahead of time. Make the tree and its creatures readily available for the children to use to recreate the story and to create their own.

THE MOON JUMPERS
by Janice May Udry, il. by Maurice Sendak (Harper, 1959).

Story: After the sun goes down and the moon comes up, an owl sitting in a pine tree awakens and the children come out to play. They dance in the grass, make up poems, and sing. When bedtime arrives, mother tells her "moon jumpers" to say goodnight to the moon.

Materials: recorded music

Directions: Ask the children to be "moon jumpers." Go outside and pretend that it's night time. Dance in the grass to recorded music. Have the children turn somersaults, hold hands and walk in a circle, pretend to climb a tree, and jump to try to touch the moon. When they begin to tire, have someone pretend to be the mother, who tells them to come inside. End with everyone saying goodnight to the moon and taking a rest.

NO JUMPING ON THE BED
by Tedd Arnold (Dial, 1987).

Story: At bedtime, Walter's father warns him not to jump on the bed, but Walter can't resist. He jumps so high that he and his bed crash through all the floors in his tall apartment building, collecting people and objects on the way. When Walter opens his eyes, he realizes he was dreaming.

Materials: boxes (big boxes are easier to work with, but shoe boxes will do), glue, scissors, markers, toy figures, paper scraps

Directions: Divide the children into groups and give each group a box to decorate like one of the rooms Walter falls through. Glue the completed boxes together to make an apartment building. Cut holes in the boxes, and have a toy figure fall through the holes. Children will want to retell the story using the props, but encourage them to create their own stories also.

NO NAP FOR BENJAMIN BADGER

by Nancy White Carlstrom, il. by Dennis Nolan (Macmillan, 1991).

Story: Benjamin Badger, nearly three years old, refuses to take a nap. Mother Badger tells him a rhyme explaining that butterflies snooze, grasshoppers rest, and young spiders nap, so he should, too. Her persuasion works well, and Benjamin nods off to sleep. (Mom does, too.)

Materials: badger puppet or stuffed badger, small stuffed mouse

Directions: Introduce the badger. Pretend he is speaking while you tell about badgers in general and about how this one dislikes taking naps. For added appeal, dress the badger in a striped shirt and overalls and let him carry a little stuffed mouse. If a stuffed badger is not available, work with a copy of Benjamin from the book and later pin it on the bulletin board. While reading this story, use lots of expression. The children will want to join in on the "No! No nap for me!" refrain. At the end of the story, yawn, close your eyes, and pretend to fall asleep. The children will be ready for a nap by this time, too.

THE PARTY

by David McPhail (Little, 1990).

Story: A father comes into his son's room to read him a bedtime story. However, the father falls asleep while reading, and the young boy and his stuffed animals have a party. The father remains oblivious to all of the noise and laughter. Finally, the party goers drag Dad off to his own bed.

Materials: stuffed animals, balloons, snack, writing materials

Directions: After reading the story, the children will want to have their own party. Write out invitations to them using the one in the book as a guideline. Supply lots of stuffed animals, or have the children bring their own from home. Use a doll for the father. Blow up some balloons and have a little snack. Then dramatize the party in the story or let the children create their own.

TEN IN A BED
by Mary Rees (Joy Street Books, 1988).

Story: There are ten little children in a bed. When the one on one end says, "Roll over! Roll over!" the one on the other end falls out, followed by another and another until only one little girl is left. She enjoys the luxury of having the bed all to herself until the others come to pull her out.

Materials: quilt, dolls (or stuffed animals)

Directions: Read the story and ask the children to join in on the refrain, "Roll over! Roll over!" Before the end of the story, the children will be repeating the entire verse along with you. Let the children reenact the story using a quilt for the bed and dolls or stuffed animals for the children. This story offers a great opportunity for a math lesson. How many fell out of bed, how many are still in bed, and so on?

WHEN EVERYONE WAS FAST ASLEEP
by Tomie de Paola (Holiday House, 1976).

Story: The Fog Maiden's cat wakens two small children and sends them into the enchanted night. In their adventure, the children meet an elf-horse, attend an extravagant ball, and watch a play at the palace. Then the Fog Maiden floats them back to their beds.

Materials: costume ball masks (see Dream Crafts), recorded waltz music

Directions: When reading, ask the children to join in on the "Tra la" song. Teach the children a few waltz steps, and have them put on the masks they made. Dramatize this dreamy story by playing dance music while the children pretend they're princes or princesses at the ball. For a special treat, serve hot buttered bread stacked on a plate with honey and a glass of milk. Refer to Dream Snacks for bread-making suggestions.

Berger, Barbara. **GRANDFATHER TWILIGHT** (Philomel, 1984).

At day's end, Grandfather Twilight takes a pearl from a wooden chest and walks along with it. As he walks, the pearl grows and grows until it's too big to carry. When he gives the pearl away, it becomes the moon.

Brown, Margaret Wise, il. by Garth Williams. **WAIT TILL THE MOON IS FULL** (Harper, 1948).

A little raccoon wants to go out into the night to see the moon, meet an owl, and see the darkness, but his mother keeps telling him he must wait until the moon is full. And that's just what he does!

Cazet, Denys. **MOTHER NIGHT** (Orchard, 1989).

Mother Night hushes the earth as night draws near. The baby animals go to sleep as Father Bear tells a story. Mother Mouse sings, Mother Raven kisses her children, and Mother Fox wishes good dreams.

Dragonwagon, Crescent, il. by Jerry Pinkney. **HALF A MOON AND ONE WHOLE STAR** (Macmillan, 1986).

As Susan falls asleep on a summer evening, the night creatures—owls, possums, and raccoons—begin to awaken and Half-a-Moon and One Whole Star appear in the night sky. The entire night world comes alive!

Edwards, Frank B. and John Bianchi. **MELODY MOONER STAYED UP ALL NIGHT!** (Firefly, 1990).

Ignoring her parents' calls that it's time for bed, Melody Mooner stays up all night. This little piglet passes the time with outlandish diversions. But after chasing sheep and visiting singing cows, she heads for her bed.

Garrison, Christian, il. by Diane Goode. **THE DREAM EATER** (Bradbury, 1978).

A small boy named Yukio dreams that a demon is chasing him. When he discovers that other villagers also suffer from nightmares, he rescues the baku, a dream eater, who eats the bad dreams, and spares the villagers.

Goode, Diane. **I HEAR A NOISE** (E. P. Dutton, 1988).

A little boy calls to his mother when he hears a noise outside his window. In the boy's imagination, a friendly monster carries both the boy and his mother away to the monster's home. However, the monster's mother makes her child monster return the boy and his mother to their own home.

Hoban, Russell, il. by Garth Williams. **BEDTIME FOR FRANCES** (Harper, 1960).

Frances is a little badger who tries nearly everything to fall asleep. She drinks a glass of milk, kisses her parents good night several times, sings an alphabet song, and pesters her parents until they become angry. Finally, Frances tires and falls fast asleep.

Issacs, Gwynne L., il. by Cathi Hepworth. **WHILE YOU ARE ASLEEP** (Walker, 1991).

While most people are asleep, others are pursuing their night jobs. Marsha works all night at the doughnut shop, Phil drives a taxi, and doctors and nurses work in the hospital.

Jam, Teddy, il. by Eric Beddows. **NIGHT CARS** (Orchard, 1989).

A baby who won't go to sleep watches out his window and views the activities of the night. There's the bustle of the taxis, the snow flurries, noisy early-morning garbage trucks, many passing cars, and walking feet.

Joyce, William. **GEORGE SHRINKS** (Scholastic, 1985).

George dreams he is small, and when he wakes up he finds it to be true. He washes the dishes by sliding on a sponge, rides on his baby brother's back, and flies his toy airplane back to his bed.

Koide, Tan, il. by Yasuko Koide. **MAY WE SLEEP HERE TONIGHT?** (Atheneum, 1983).

While hiking, three lost gophers enter a warm, unoccupied home. Two bunnies join them, followed by three raccoons. When they are all settled down for the night in the bed, the door opens and Mr. Bear, the owner of the home, comes in. Fortunately, he is friendly and all ends well.

Lester, Alison. **RUBY** (Houghton Mifflin, 1988).

Betsy is Ruby's quilt and best friend. Late one night in Ruby's dream, Betsy lifts Ruby into the air and takes her to an island where they rescue lion cubs for the king. At dawn, the two return home from their adventure.

Lindberg, Reeve, il. by Steven Kellogg. **THE DAY THE GOOSE GOT LOOSE** (Dial, 1990).

One day on the farm, the goose gets loose. Then the bull breaks through the fence, the ram knocks a neighbor into the air, and the horses gallop all over town. That night, the children dream of the day's adventures.

Morgenstern, Constance, il. by Cat Bowman. **GOOD NIGHT, FEET** (Holt, 1991).

A child says good night in rhyme to the different parts of his body—feet, hands, mouth, ears, and eyes—as he recounts the adventures of the day. After he says goodnight to himself, he falls asleep.

Rice, Eve, il. by Peter Sis. **CITY NIGHT** (Greenwillow, 1987).

In this illustrated rhyme, the beauty of the city at night is depicted through the eyes of a little girl. As the clock ticks, the girl goes to bed, but first she says good night to her pet bird and her parents. Another book by the same author is **GOOD NIGHT, GOOD NIGHT.**

Ringgold, Faith. **TAR BEACH** (Crown, 1991).

A young girl up on "tar beach," the rooftop of her Harlem apartment, dreams about how wonderful it would be if she were free to go wherever she felt like going. The stars lift her up and she flies above the George Washington Bridge and other wonderful sights of the city.

Ryder, Joanne, il. by Amy Schwartz. **THE NIGHT FLIGHT** (Four Winds, 1985).

After Anna falls asleep, she dreams of flying to her favorite park. Here, the fish whisper to her and she has an adventure with a friendly lion.

Ryder, Joanne, il. by Dennis Nolan. **STEP INTO THE NIGHT** (Four Winds, 1988).

In the evening, a child steps outside her home and imagines the lives of the night creatures. A mouse creeps along to find berries, a spider builds her sticky web, and fireflies flash this way and that. The child is in awe of the happenings in the night until the lights of her home beckon her back.

Rylant, Cynthia, il. by Mary Szilagyi. **NIGHT IN THE COUNTRY** (Bradbury, 1986).

Nighttime in the country is very dark. The owls swoop, rabbits patter about, a river flows, and the animals in the barn roll over. Toward morning, a bird is the first to notice that night in the country is ending.

Sage, James, il. by Warwick Hutton. **TO SLEEP** (Atheneum, 1990).

In a quiet conversation, a mother explains to her child why it's time to go to bed. She says that it's the end of the day, and night has fallen, the time for rest. Soon the child lays his head on his pillow and falls asleep.

Salter, Mary Jo, il. by Stacy Schuett. **THE MOON COMES HOME** (Knopf, 1989).

A child thinks that the moon floating above her grandmother's house is following her home. It turns the corner with her, passes the same streets and woods, and never gets lost. The moon even peeks in the child's bedroom window and watches as she falls asleep.

Seuss, Dr. **DR. SEUSS'S SLEEP BOOK** (Random House, 1962).

In this hilarious adventure, a small bug named Van Vleck yawns. His yawns spread as everything falls asleep. A super machine counts all of the sleepers as they nod off, and finally it's time for the reader to join the others in sleep.

Shepperson, Robert. **THE SANDMAN** (Farrar, 1989).

One night, Jay stays awake to see if the mythical sandman really does come to sprinkle sand on his eyes. Sure enough, the sandman arrives with a wheelbarrow of magic sand. The fun begins as the sandman attempts to rock Jay to sleep. He reads Jay a story, they share a bedtime snack together, and then they sing lullabies until dawn arrives.

Spier, Peter. **DREAMS** (Doubleday, 1986).

In this nearly wordless book, two children play with their dogs on a warm summer day. They look into the sky and dream. The clouds appear to be animals, sailing ships, and giant fish.

Wiesner, David. **FREE FALL** (Lothrop, 1988).

In this wordless book, a young boy dreams of daring adventures inspired by the things in his bedroom. He conquers a dragon, travels to enchanted lands, and floats free into a new day.

Zemach-Bersin, Kaethe. **THE FUNNY DREAM** (Greenway, 1988).

A young child dreams that she has grown big and her parents have become small. Her parents are messy and stubborn as the child gets them washed, dressed, fed, and ready for school. When she wakes up, she's glad to find it's a normal day.

Ziefert, Harriet. **GOOD NIGHT EVERYONE!** (Little, 1988).

Before Harry goes to sleep, he settles all his toys in their special places for the night and says, "Good night everyone." Then Harry falls asleep, but the toys get up to play.

Ziefert, Harriet, il. by Mavis Smith. **I WANT TO SLEEP IN YOUR BED!** (Harper & Row, 1990).

When nighttime arrives, the parakeet, dog, Susan's little brother, and her parents are all asleep, but Susan is at her parents' door saying she wants to sleep in their bed. Finally, Susan is so tired she falls asleep.

Zolotow, Charlotte, il. by Ilse Plume. **SLEEPY BOOK** (Harper, 1988).

In this poetic text, each animal sleeps in its own special way. Bears sleep in dark caves, kittens sleep in the sun, and cranes sleep standing on one leg. And, of course, little girls and boys sleep in their warm, cozy beds.

✦ Dream Poems and Songs ✦

WEE WILLIE WINKIE

Wee Willie Winkie runs through the town,
Upstairs and downstairs in his nightgown,
Rapping at the window, crying through
    the lock,
Are the children all in bed, for now it's
    eight o'clock?
—Mother Goose

DIDDLE, DIDDLE DUMPLING, MY SON JOHN

Diddle, diddle dumpling, my son John,
Went to bed with his trousers on;
One shoe off, and one shoe on,
Diddle, diddle dumpling, my son John.
—Mother Goose

THE MAN IN THE MOON

The Man in the Moon looked out of the
    moon,
Looked out of the moon and said,
"'Tis time for all children on the earth
To think about getting to bed!"
—Mother Goose

THE MOON IS OUT TONIGHT

The moon is out tonight.
(Make circle with arms.)
The stars are shining bright.
(Wiggle fingers overhead.)
My mom says it's time for bed.
(Rest head on hands.)
And she's right, "Good night."

GOOD NIGHT

The moon is peeking in my window.
(Make circle with arms.)
The stars light up my room.
(Wiggle fingers overhead.)
I feel the gentle breeze.
(Blow softly.)
And know it's time to say, "Good night."

WHERE IS SLEEPYHEAD?

(Tune: "Where Is Thumbkin?")

Where is sleepyhead?
Where is sleepyhead?
(Put hands behind back.)
Here I am.
(Bring out one hand holding up index
    finger.)
Here I am.
(Repeat using the other hand.)
How are you today, dear?
(Wiggle one finger.)
Very well, I thank you.
(Wiggle the other finger.)
Go to bed, go to bed.
(Put hands behind back again.)

More Dream Poems and Songs

"Night Time," p. 67, "Sleepy," p. 82 in
RING A RING O'ROSES: FINGER PLAYS
FOR PRE-SCHOOL CHILDREN (Flint Public
Library, 1988).

"Hush, Little Baby," p. 181, "Twinkle,
Twinkle, Little Star," p. 202, "Rock-a-Bye
Baby," p. 221, and "Are You Sleeping?",
p. 234 in READER'S DIGEST CHILDREN'S
SONG BOOK (Reader's Digest General
Books, 1985).

"All the Pretty Little Horses," p. 52 in WEE
SING by Pamela Conn Beall and Susan
Hagen Nipp (Price/Stern/Sloan, 1982).

"Slippery Sam," p. 45, "Bedtime" and
"Hushabye My Darling," p. 70, and
"Good Night, Good Night," p. 88 in
READ-ALOUD RHYMES FOR THE VERY
YOUNG, selected by Jack Prelutsky, il. by
Marc Brown (Knopf, 1986).

SONGS THE SANDMAN SINGS: A
Collection of Poems to be Read at
Bedtime, compiled by Gwendolyn
Reed, il. by Peggy Owens Skillen
(Atheneum, 1969).

⭐ Dream Games and Dramatic Play ⭐

SANDMAN TAG

Designate boundaries for playing this game. One child pretends to be the sandman. He or she tags the other children and then pretends to sprinkle sand in their eyes. Then they must fall asleep. Each time this game is played, choose a different child to be the sandman. This is a great game to play before nap time!

WHO'S GOT THE PEARL?

After reading GRANDFATHER TWILIGHT, play this game. (It's similar to "Button, Button, Who's Got the Button," except a costume jewelry pearl is substituted for a button.) The children sit in a circle with their hands placed together. The child chosen to be Grandfather Twilight holds the pearl in his or her hands.

Grandfather Twilight moves around the circle pretending to drop the pearl into each player's hand, but actually dropping it in only one player's hand. After going around the circle, Grandfather Twilight asks, "Pearl, pearl, who's got my pearl?" All the children attempt to guess who's holding the pearl. The player who guesses correctly is the next Grandfather Twilight. Play until everyone has had a chance to be Grandfather Twilight.

GOOD NIGHT, OWL

After reading GOOD NIGHT, OWL, the children will enjoy dramatizing it. Designate an area in the room for an imaginary tree. Ask one child to be the owl who pretends to sit in the tree. All the other children pretend to be the other tree inhabitants. Several children can be the same creature to make sure that everyone has a part. The first time this is done, an adult may assist by reading the story as the players act and make the sounds, but eventually the children will be able to do the dramatization with little guidance. This game develops independence and leadership.

GOOD NIGHT, BODY

The children sit in a circle with their legs pointed toward the middle. One child says "Good night" to some part of his or her body (head, nose, foot, etc.). The other children join in whispering "Good night" to the same part of their body. One at a time, other children say "Good night" to another part of their body, with the rest of the group joining in, until all body parts have been wished "Good night."

Good night, toes.

FLYING BOAT

Materials: boat pattern, colored tag board, scissors, markers or crayons, stapler, string

Directions: After reading THE DREAM CHILD, the children will want to make their own flying boats. Use the pattern provided to cut out the boat pieces from lightweight tag board. Let the children color the boats if desired. Help them fold over the end pieces slightly and staple together. Cut slits in the boat and insert the wings or use staples. Help the children attach two strings, one at each end, to hang their boat from the ceiling. The children may draw and cut out their own dream child or draw themselves flying in the boat. The flying boat may also be made from a cardboard milk carton by spray-painting the carton and attaching the wings. A larger version can be made and a toy doll or stuffed animal placed in the boat. The children will want to tell visitors about their flying boats and relate what adventures they intend to encounter.

NIGHT SKY

Materials: moon and star patterns, yellow and white paper, string, glue, sparkles, scissors, markers or crayons

Directions: To create a night sky in the room, enlarge the moon and star patterns provided. Cut a moon and stars from yellow and white paper. Draw the facial features on the moon. Spread glue on the stars and cover with sparkles. Attach strings and hang from the ceiling at various lengths. Let older children create their own stars and moon to bring home.

If you want to make the sky more authentic, cut out one large moon and several smaller stars. Arrange the stars in a few familiar constellations (the Big Dipper, Little Dipper, etc.). Remember to make one big star for the North Star.

QUILT

Materials: quilt patterns, colored paper and paper scraps, scissors, glue, sheets of paper

Directions: Enlarge the pattern pieces to the desired size. Provide pre-cut pieces of colored paper scraps for each child to glue onto a sheet of paper. Let the children choose the colors they want to use.

Older children may create their own quilt patterns and pin the pieces together on the wall to make one big quilt. Colored markers or crayons may be used to decorate the quilt.

If possible, show children a real quilt ahead of time, and talk about how fabric quilts are made. This project will be especially meaningful after reading RUBY by Alison Lester.

COSTUME BALL MASK

Materials: mask pattern, lightweight colored tag board, scissors, tape, 12-inch dowel stick, colored markers or crayons

Directions: Use the pattern to cut out masks from tag board. Help the children cut out the eyes. Encourage them to draw facial features using the provided designs as a guideline. Or let the children glue on yarn, macaroni, lace, feathers, or sequins. Show the children how to tape a dowel stick to the back of their mask for the final touch. Use the masks in conjunction with WHEN EVERYONE WAS FAST ASLEEP. Refer to Read-Aloud Stories for additional ideas.

PAPER MOUSE

Materials: mouse pattern, pink yarn, glue, black marker, scissors, pink and white paper

Directions: After reading Jack Keats' DREAMS, the children will want to make their own paper mice. Make copies of the mouse pattern and cut out on the fold to make the mice stand up. Have the children glue on pink ears and a yarn tail, then draw in features. To make a mouse similar to the one in the story, make a cone for the head and one for the body and glue or tape them together. Glue on ears and a tail and draw in features.

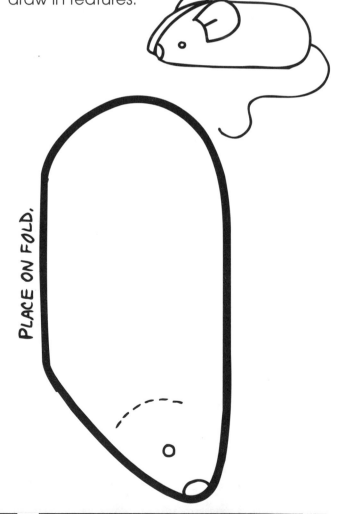

PLACE ON FOLD.

Boat Pattern

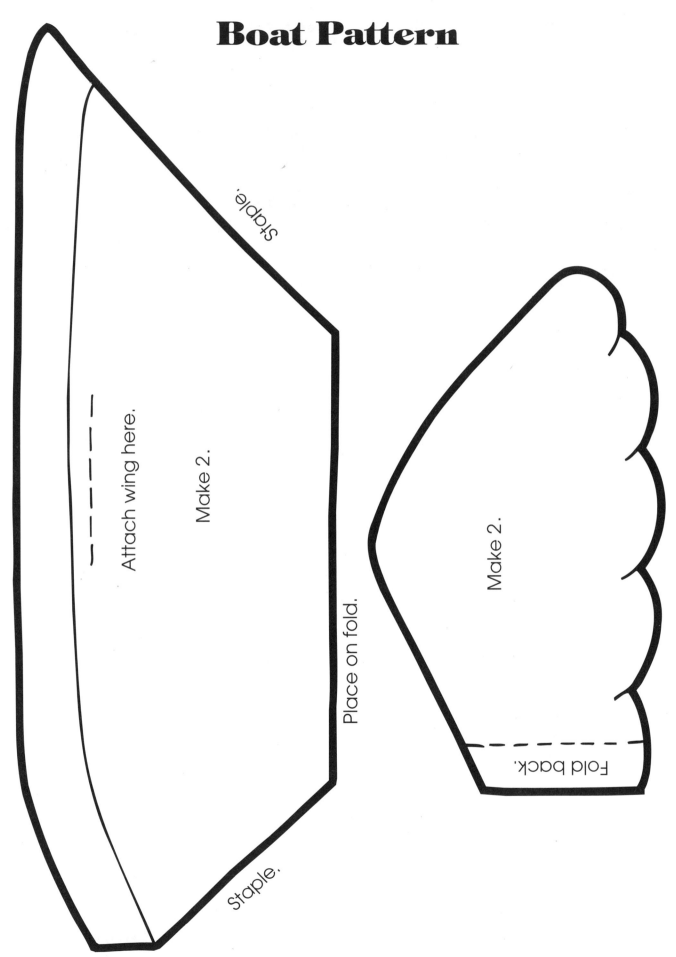

Staple.

Attach wing here.

Make 2.

Place on fold.

Staple.

Make 2.

Fold back.

Moon and Star Patterns

Quilt Patterns

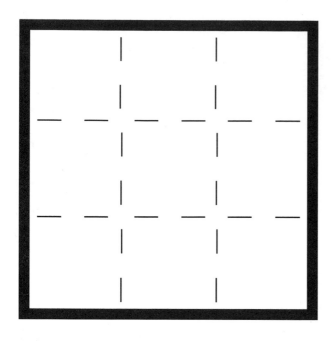

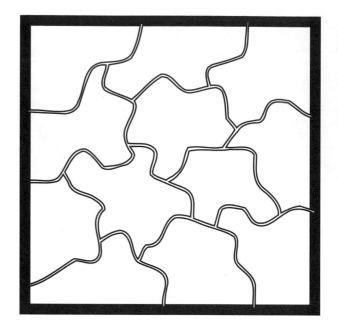

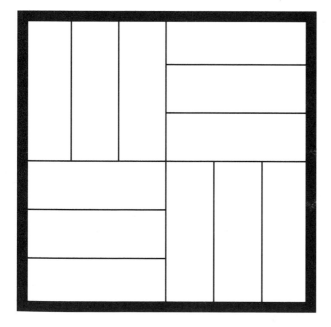

Mask Pattern

HOMEMADE BREAD

After reading WHEN EVERYONE WAS FAST ASLEEP, use hot roll mixes to make several loaves of bread. (This is a good time to recruit some volunteer help.) Divide the children into groups so that each child can participate in the mixing and kneading. Shape the dough into loaves and bake at 425 degrees for 30 minutes. If possible, eat the bread while warm and serve with butter, honey, and milk.

MOONS MADE OF CHEESE

Use the moon pattern provided to make a cardboard pattern. Place the pattern on a slice of cheese and cut it out to make a "cheese moon." Thick cheese works best. Make indentions for the eye and mouth. Repeat so that each child receives a moon. Show the children that sometimes the moon really is made of cheese!

SLEEPING DOG
(makes one serving)

1 wiener
1/2 hot dog bun
1 slice of cheese
butter

Place a cooked wiener on a buttered hot dog bun. Top with the slice of cheese, covering all but one end of the wiener—this end serves as the head. Fold one corner of the cheese back as if folding a blanket. Bake in a 400 degree oven for 6 to 8 minutes or microwave for one minute until cheese is slightly melted.

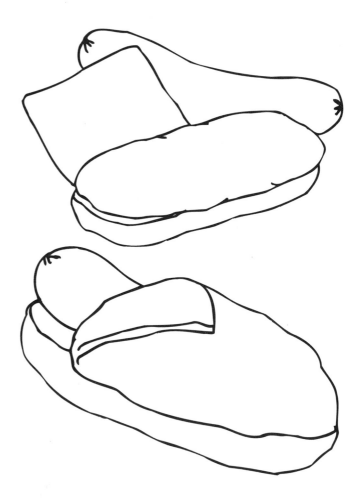

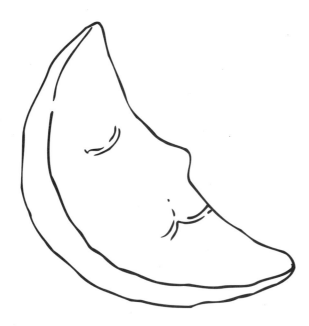

Folk tales are stories that were told and retold, passed from generation to generation, before the availability of books. They reflect the culture of the time. Fairy tales are folk tales that take place in enchanted worlds, often with human main characters. Reading both types of stories will allow children to see how our literature has evolved.

Authors and illustrators of modern children's books sometimes look to the past for inspiration. This results in the recreation of popular folk and fairy tales of yesteryear, and books that are often more suitable and appealing to a new generation. Scholastic is one publishing company that has several easy-to-read folk tales in paperback, perfect for young children. Paul Galdone, Steven Kellogg, and James Marshall have all retold many tales, modernizing some of them in delightful ways. You will find many different versions of the same tales, and it's fun to read a sampling to spot the changes.

Modernized tales often have new twists on the old stories. For example, children will love to hear the well-known tale of the three little pigs told for the first time from the wolf's point of view! These revised stories may stimulate children to create their own versions of the tales.

SETTING THE STAGE

Make a sign that says "Welcome to the Land of Folk and Fairy Tales" and post it in the reading corner. Provide an assortment of tales for the children to read or view. If stuffed folk tale characters are available, set them in the corner for the children to read to.

Enlarge and copy a variety of folk tale character illustrations to put on the walls around the room. Try using some of the less familiar characters to create an interest in tales the children may not have heard.

Make Jack's beanstalk by taping construction paper leaves and a stalk up a wall toward the ceiling. Nearby, place a sign that reads "To the Castle" with an arrow pointing up. Each child can have his or her own personal beanstalk by planting beans in a dirt-filled paper cup. Give the children the responsibility of caring for and watering their plants. The beans will sprout sooner if soaked in water first. Children will enjoy keeping track of their plant's growth.

BULLETIN BOARD IDEAS

1. Enlarge and color the "Take Time to Read" poster. For a three-dimensional effect, make the beanstalk separately from green paper and glue onto the poster. Likewise, make Jack and his book from different pieces of colored paper and attach to the beanstalk.

2. Title the bulletin board "My Favorite Folk Tale Character." Ask the children to each draw a favorite character to pin on the board.

3. Make a list of the folk and fairy tales you intend to read. Write each title on an individual strip of paper. Decorate a large envelope to look like a book cover with the title "Fantastic Folk and Fairy Tales." Place the title strips into the envelope. When it's story time, let the children take turns pulling out a title to be read. Once the tale has been read, pin the title onto the bulletin board. It will be easy for the children to see how many tales they've heard.

THE GREEDY OLD FAT MAN
retold and il. by Paul Galdone (Clarion, 1983).

Story: In this adaptation of an American folk tale, a greedy old fat man captures and eats everything in sight. He eats a little girl and boy, a cat, a dog, a fox, and some rabbits. Luckily, a clever squirrel tricks the old man and frees all the captives.

Materials: pillow, flannel board, poster paper, scissors, markers or crayons, glue, flannel or felt pieces

Directions: Without the children seeing you, slip a pillow under your shirt to make you look like the greedy old fat man. Show the illustrations while you read the tale. Ask the children to join in on the phrase, "Old man, what makes you so fat?" The children will soon join in on all of the repetitive phrases. Make flannel board characters by copying the illustrations from the book onto poster paper. Color, cut out, and glue flannel or felt onto the back of each. Make the old man big enough so that all the characters can fit underneath him as they are eaten. Allow the children to use the flannel board and characters to retell the story. Refer to the Folk and Fairy Tale Dramatic Play section for additional ideas related to the tale.

THE MITTEN
retold by Alvin Tresselt, il. by Yaroslava (Lothrop, 1964).

Story: One very cold day, a little boy loses his yellow mitten in the snow while gathering firewood. Magically, his mitten houses many forest creatures: a mouse, a frog, a rabbit, an owl, a fox, a wolf, a wild boar, and a bear. When a tired old cricket crowds into the mitten, the seams pop open and all the animals fall into the snow and scamper away.

Materials: mitten (see Folk and Fairy Tale Crafts), toy animals

Directions: Fill the big yellow mitten with the toy animals. After telling the tale, show the children the mitten, open it, and let all the creatures fall onto the floor. Ask a few children to assist you by putting the creatures back into the mitten as everyone helps retell the tale. You may want to adapt the tale to match the animals you have.

THE PRINCESS AND THE PEA

adapted and il. by Janet Stevens (Holiday House, 1982).

Story: The lion queen travels abroad with her son in search of a suitable princess for him to marry. None can be found. After returning home, a girl tiger comes to the castle, claiming to be a real princess. While sleeping, the tiger feels a pea through 20 mattresses and 20 feather beds. This proves that she really is a princess, and she marries the prince.

Materials: pea on pillows (see Folk and Fairy Tale Crafts), small mattresses or blankets, dried peas

Directions: Read different versions of this tale to illustrate how the same tale can vary. Provide several small mattresses or blankets and a few dried peas for the children to use while acting out the tale. Encourage the children to create their own versions. Let each child take home the pea-on-a-pillow craft he or she made to use when retelling the tale to parents.

RAPUNZEL

retold by Bernice Chardiet, il. by Julie Downing (Scholastic, 1990).

Story: A powerful witch hides beautiful Rapunzel in a high tower. Rapunzel lets down her long hair and a prince climbs up her golden tresses and into the tower. Rapunzel and the prince fall in love, but the wicked witch tries to destroy them. Luckily love wins out, and Rapunzel and her prince live happily ever after.

Materials: poster paper, marker, yellow yarn, toy prince or illustration of the prince, sign, tape, glue, scissors

Directions: Draw a tall tower on poster paper, cut out, and attach to a wall. Glue long strands of yellow yarn (Rapunzel's hair) to the tower. Make a photocopy of the prince from the book (or use a toy prince) to attach to the yarn as if he is climbing up. Nearby, post a sign saying, "Rapunzel, Rapunzel! Let down your hair!" Post the display a few days before telling the tale to arouse curiosity.

RUM PUM PUM

(A folk tale from India)
retold by Maggie Duff, il. by Jose Aruego and Ariane Dewey (Macmillan, 1978).

Story: Blackbird beats his drum as he goes to make war on the king who has stolen Blackbird's wife. Along the way, Cat, Stick, River, and the ants join in the successful battle against the king.

Materials: kettledrum (see Folk and Fairy Tale Crafts)

Directions: Use a real or homemade kettledrum to play when Blackbird plays his drum in the tale. The children can join in by repeating the refrain "Rum pum pum." If possible, borrow a kettledrum from the music department and ask a student or teacher to demonstrate how to play it. Let each child play the drum, then make their own drum to use when retelling the tale.

THUMBELINA

retold by Amy Ehrlich, il. by Susan Jeffers (Dial, 1979).

Story: In this classic tale by Hans Christian Anderson, a lonely woman wishes for a child. Her dream comes true when she finds a tiny girl in the petals of a flower. The child is the size of the woman's thumb, so she names her Thumbelina. Thumbelina's adventures lead her to the small flower people where she receives a beautiful pair of wings that enable her to dart among the flowers.

Materials: Thumbelina doll (directions follow), silk flower

Directions: Make a simple Thumbelina doll by stuffing a piece of flesh-colored fabric and tying it with a string to make the head. Draw on features. Glue a bit of fabric to the head for a scarf and to the body for a skirt. Place Thumbelina on a flower with movable petals and close up the petals to conceal her. Begin telling the story using the flower as a prop, opening the petals one by one to reveal Thumbelina. Read the rest of the tale, paraphrasing as necessary for young children.

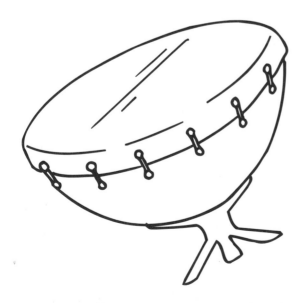

THE TOWN MOUSE AND THE COUNTRY MOUSE

adapted and il. by Janet Stevens
(Holiday House, 1987).

Story: In this humorous fable, a town mouse visits his cousin, a country mouse.

Materials: mouse stick puppets (directions follow), cheese

Directions: To make puppets, copy the two mice illustrations onto poster paper, color, cut out, and attach them to sticks. Introduce the two mice to the children by letting the mice talk to each other about themselves. The children might like to ask the mice questions. After reading the tale, provide a healthy cheese snack for your little "mice students."

THE TURNIP

il. by Pierr Morgan (Philomel, 1990).

Story: This old Russian folk tale is retold using delightful Russian names. Dedoushka can't pull up the turnip. Baboushka, Mashenka, Geouchka, and Keska all come to help without success. Luckily, a little field mouse lends a hand, and up comes the turnip.

Materials: large paper turnip (see Folk and Fairy Tale Crafts)

Directions: Set the giant turnip on the floor. Use lots of expression while reading this tale—be sad and shake your head when the turnip won't come up, and call out loudly when asking the various characters to come to help. Ask the children to repeat the repetitive phrases with you as you read. Refer to Folk and Fairy Tale Dramatic Play for further suggestions concerning this tale.

Aardema, Verna, il. by Petra Mathers. **BORREQUITA AND THE COYOTE** (Knopf, 1991).

A coyote wants to eat Borrequita, a little lamb, but each time Borrequita outwits the coyote. First, Borrequita leaves the coyote holding up a mountain so that she can escape. Then she strikes the coyote's mouth so hard that he runs away and never bothers her again.

Aardema, Verna, il. by Jerry Pinkney. **RABBIT MAKES A MONKEY OF LION** (Dial, 1989).

Rabbit and her friends, Bush-rat and Turtle, enjoy eating honey from the calabash tree. A dimwitted lion tries to capture them by saying that the honey belongs to him. Luckily, the three are able to outsmart the lion.

Appleby, Ellen. **THE THREE BILLY GOATS GRUFF** (Scholastic, 1984).

These colorful illustrations breathe new excitement into the familiar tale of the three goats who triumph over a scary troll.

Asbjornsen, P. C. and Jorgen Moe, il. by Svend Otto S. **THE RUNAWAY PANCAKE** (Larousse, 1980).

A mother cooks a fat pancake for her seven hungry children, but when it's done, it hops out of the pan and runs away. The pancake outruns the mother, the grandfather, the children, and all the other characters along the way. Finally, a pig tricks the pancake and eats it.

Berenzy, Alix. **A FROG PRINCE** (Holt, 1989).

This traditional tale is told with a twist. The frog goes on a journey to find a true princess after he's been rejected by the princess whose golden ball he retrieved. On the search, the frog encounters grave dangers and great obstacles, but when he's about to give up he finds his worthy bride.

Brett, Jan. **THE BEAUTY AND THE BEAST** (Clarion, 1989).

When Beauty goes to visit the Beast, she is very frightened until she discovers that he is kind and compassionate. Beast falls in love with Beauty and wants her to become his wife. When she agrees, the spell is broken and Beast turns into a handsome prince.

Brett, Jan. **THE MITTEN** (G.P. Putnam's Sons, 1989).

Nicki drops one of his white mittens in the snow. The woodland animals find it and crawl in: a curious mole, a rabbit, a hedgehog, an owl, a badger, a shy fox, and a great bear. Then a little mouse crawls onto the bear's nose and makes the bear sneeze. All of the animals fall into the snow, Nicki's mitten flies into the air, and he retrieves it.

Briggs, Raymond. **JIM AND THE BEANSTALK** (Coward-McCann, 1970).

Jim climbs an unusually large plant he finds growing past his window. At the top, he discovers a castle and a giant. The giant is not an ordinary frightening giant. This one needs a pair of glasses, some hair, and a new set of teeth. Jim is able to help the giant, and the two become good friends.

Ehrlich, Amy, il. by Susan Jeffers. **THE WILD SWANS** (Dial, 1981).

In this Hans Christian Anderson tale, 11 princes are changed into wild swans. Their only sister, Elsie, tries to rescue them, but comes into trouble herself. The wild swans save Elsie and become princes again.

Galdone, Joanna, il. by Paul Galdone. **THE LITTLE GIRL AND THE BIG BEAR** (Houghton Mifflin/Clarion, 1980).

A little girl loses her way in the woods while picking berries. A huge bear holds her captive in his hut and turns her into his servant. But the clever girl outwits the bear by hiding in a basket of pies, and she returns safely to her grandparents' house.

Galdone, Paul. **THE ELVES AND THE SHOEMAKER** (Clarion, 1984).

A poor shoemaker and his wife discover two little naked elves are helping them by making shoes during the night. In return, the shoemaker and his wife sew fine clothes for the little elves.

Galdone, Paul. **THE GINGERBREAD BOY** (Clarion, 1975).

A little old lady bakes a gingerbread boy, but when she opens the oven he pops out and runs away. He eludes the hungry grasp of everyone until he happens upon a fox who is even more clever than the gingerbread boy.

Grimm, The Brothers, il. by Mark Corcoran. **BRAVE LITTLE TAILOR** (Troll, 1977).

A tailor kills seven flies in one blow, but when he tells of this accomplishment he gives the impression that he's killed seven men, not flies. The tailor manages to outwit the giants in the forest and gains a reputation for being very brave. His glory allows him to win the princess' hand in marriage.

Grimm, The Brothers, il. by Eugen Sopko. **THE FALLING STARS** (Holt, 1985).

A little girl is all alone in the world. Her only possessions are the clothes she's wearing and a small piece of bread. As the girl wanders out into the world, she gives away the bread and her clothes to those in need. But her compassion is rewarded because stars fall and turn into gold coins, providing her with enough money for the rest of her life.

Grimm, The Brothers, il. by Lisbeth Zwerger. **THE SEVEN RAVENS** (Morrow, 1981).

A father's hastily spoken words doom his seven sons to live as ravens. Their sister walks to the end of the world where she finally finds her brothers and is able to set them free. They all joyfully return home.

Grimm, The Brothers, il. by Errol LeCain. **THORN ROSE** (Puffin, 1981).

This memorable fairy tale about a sleeping beauty has been condensed into an appropriate length for young children. The illustrations help tell the tale: Thorn Rose, a beautiful princess, sleeps for 100 years after a spell is cast upon her. She doesn't wake up until the kiss of a prince breaks the spell.

Grimm, The Brothers, il. by Martin Ursell.
THE WOLF AND THE SEVEN LITTLE KIDS
(Silver Burdett, 1986).

Nanny goat warns her seven little kids to beware of the wolf while she is away in search of food. However, the clever wolf fools the little kids and manages to eat six of them. When the full wolf stops to rest on his way home, Nanny goat cuts open the wolf's stomach and rescues her little kids.

Gross, Ruth Belov, il. by Winslow Pinney Pels. **HANSEL AND GRETEL** (Scholastic, 1988).

Hansel and Gretel live near a big forest with their woodcutter father and step-mother. When there isn't enough food for all of them, Hansel and Gretel are abandoned deep in the forest. The children are held captive by an evil witch who lives in a gingerbread house. Eventually, they escape and return home safely. (James Marshall has also written a wonderful Hansel and Gretel tale.)

Harper, Wilhelmina, il. by William Wiesner. **THE GUNNIWOLF** (Dutton, 1967).

Little Girl's mother cautions her to stay away from the jungle. However, one day she accidentally wanders into the jungle while picking flowers. Though Little Girl meets up with the gunniwolf, she's able to fool him and escape to her home.

Heine, Helme. **PRINCE BEAR** (McElderry, 1987).

In this German fairy tale, every bear can change into a prince and every princess can change into a bear. But when men invade the land and cut down forests and build highways, the happy balance is upset, and bears, princes, and princesses can no longer trade places.

Hewitt, Kathryn. **THE THREE SILLIES** (Harcourt Brace, 1986).

In this English tale, a young man believes his sweetheart and her family are the silliest people in the world. He finds them all weeping because they are afraid an ax stuck in the ceiling might fall and injure their future baby if the man and his sweetheart should marry. The young man travels around the world until he meets three others who are even sillier than his beloved and her family. Happily, he returns home to marry his silly sweetheart.

Huck, Charlotte, il. by Anita Lobel. **PRINCESS FURBALL** (Greenwillow, 1989).

In this variation on the Cinderella theme, the princess escapes from the cruel king who betrothed her to an ogre in exchange for 50 wagons of silver. The princess dresses in a coat of 1,000 furs and uses her own ingenuity, rather than relying on a fairy godmother, to win her happiness and marriage to a kind prince.

Jacobs, Joseph, il. by Margot Tomes. **TATTERCOATS** (Putnam, 1989).

A rich old lord has only one little granddaughter, but he refuses to see her because his favorite daughter died at the granddaughter's birth. The granddaughter is called Tattercoats because she's so poorly dressed. Her only friends are her old nurse and the gooseherd. When the prince falls in love with Tattercoats at the king's ball, they marry, and Tattercoats is no longer unhappy.

Karlin, Barbara, il. by James Marshall. **CINDERELLA** (Little, Brown, 1989).

This Cinderella tale is delightfully different. It's told in a fresh and funny manner with witty characters portrayed by the illustrator. The tale ends with Cinderella's family moving into the palace; Cinderella finding a lord of the court to marry her vulgar stepsisters; and the fairy godmother moving in just to be sure that everyone really does live happily ever after.

Kellogg, Steven. **CHICKEN LITTLE** (Morrow, 1985).

In this updated story, Chicken Little and her friends form a chain-reaction panic when they believe the sky is falling. Together they go to tell the police. Foxy Loxy disguises himself as a policeman, but justice wins and Foxy Loxy is sent to prison. Chicken Little plants the acorn and it grows into a beautiful oak tree.

Langton, Jane, il. by Ilse Plume. **THE HEDGEHOG BOY** (Harper & Row, 1985).

In this Latvian tale, the Forest Mother gives an old childless couple a special basket. Inside is a baby boy covered with sharp prickles like a hedgehog. He is a good boy and the couple love him. One day, as the boy tends his father's pigs, he saves the life of a princess. The hedgehog boy marries the princess and eventually turns into a handsome young man.

Lindgren, Astrid, il. by Harald Wiberg. **THE TOMTEN** (Coward-McCann, 1961).

The Tomten, a kindly old troll of Swedish folklore, lives in a corner of the hayloft. He comes out at night in the snowy winter to guard over the people and creatures on the farm. No one has ever seen him, but all know he's there.

Lindgren, Astrid, il. by Harald Wiberg. **THE TOMTEN AND THE FOX** (Coward-McCann, 1965).

On a quiet winter night, a hungry fox silently creeps to the farm to find something to eat. The people in the farmhouse don't see him, but the Tomten does. After the Tomten gives the fox porridge to eat, the fox walks away satisfied and happy.

Littledale, Freya, il. by Troy Howell. **PETER AND THE NORTH WIND** (Scholastic, 1988).

Peter goes to the barn to get flour, but the North Wind blows the flour away. When Peter complains, the North Wind grants Peter and his mother a magic cloth and goat, which are stolen by an innkeeper. Peter is then granted a magic stick which beats the innkeeper until he returns the cloth and goat.

Marshall, James. **GOLDILOCKS AND THE THREE BEARS** (Dial, 1988).

In this updated version, Goldilocks visits the bears' Victorian home while the bears are out riding bicycles. Goldilocks creates pandemonium with the porridge, chairs, and beds before escaping out a window when the bears return.

Marshall, James. **RED RIDING HOOD** (Dial, 1987).

Red Riding Hood takes custard to her ill granny. On the way, she meets a charming and mannerly wolf who offers to escort her safely through the woods. When they arrive at Granny's house, the wolf eats both Granny and Red Riding Hood. Luckily, a hunter kills the wolf, cuts him open, and frees the two. Red Riding Hood decides that she will never speak to strangers again, no matter how charming they appear.

Martin, Rafe, il. by Ed Young. **FOOLISH RABBIT'S BIG MISTAKE** (Putnam, 1985).

A foolish rabbit believes the loud crash he hears is the sound of the earth breaking up. He hurries off in a panic to warn two other rabbits, two bears, an elephant, and some snakes. A lion finally brings the frightened animals to their senses.

McQueen, Lucinda. **THE LITTLE RED HEN** (Scholastic, 1985).

In this lesson about sharing responsibilities and chores, the goose, the cat, and the dog will not help the little red hen make bread. They won't help plant the wheat, care for it, thresh it, take it to the mill, or bake the bread. But they all want to help her eat the bread. The little red hen says that since she did all the work herself, she gets to eat the bread herself. Available as a Big Book.

Morris, Winifred, il. by Friso Henstra. **THE FUTURE OF YEN-TZU** (Atheneum, 1992).

In this traditional Chinese tale, the youngest son of a poor farmer sets out to seek his destiny. He's mistaken for a famous wise man and wins the favor of the Emperor when his misunderstood advice averts a war.

Perrault, Charles, il. by Fred Marcellino. **PUSS IN BOOTS** (Farrar, Straus & Giroux, 1990).

This 300-year-old story tells the adventures of the miller's youngest son and his rascal cat, Puss. The son gives Puss a sack and a pair of boots. Puss outwits everyone in an adventure that ends with the marriage of his master and the princess.

Pevear, Richard, il. by Robert Rayevsky. **MISTER CAT-AND-A-HALF** (Macmillan, 1987).

In this Ukrainian tale, a wolf, a bear, and a hare want to marry Mistress Fox, but she's already married to Mister Cat-and-a-half. Mistress Fox tricks all of the animals into inviting her husband to dinner.

Plume, Ilse. **THE BREMEN TOWN MUSICIANS** (Doubleday, 1980).

A donkey, a dog, a cat, and a rooster all grow too old to be useful to their masters, so they set out for Bremen Town to become musicians. Along the way, they see a cozy cottage that would be a wonderful place to settle. But first they must chase away the band of robbers already inside.

Prokofiev, Sergei, il. by Charles Mikolaycak. **PETER AND THE WOLF** (Viking, 1982).

In this orchestral fairy tale, Peter ignores his grandfather's warnings not to go beyond the gate out into the big green meadow where a wolf lives. The wolf devours a duck, but, fortunately, Peter captures the wolf. Also available with recorded music.

Ross, Tony. **LAZY JACK** (Dial, 1986).

In this funny fairy tale, Jack is the laziest person in the whole world. His mother insists he go out to get a job, and this is the start of many misadventures. On the first day at work, Jack earns a gold coin, but he loses it on his way home. His mother tells him to put his pay in his pocket the next time. But, the next day his pay is milk, which he puts in his pocket—and that's the way it goes. However, when Jack carries a donkey on his back, he makes the sad princess laugh and he wins her hand in marriage.

Folk and Fairy Tale Poems and Songs

Here are a couple of variations of popular rhymes which have become a part of our folklore.

HUMPTY DUMPTY

Humpty Dumpty sat on a wall,
Humpty Dumpty had a great fall,
All the king's horses and all the king's
    men
Had scrambled eggs for breakfast
    again.
—Anonymous

MARY HAD A LITTLE LAMB

Mary had a little lamb,
You've heard this tale before;
But did you know
She passed her plate
And had a little more.
—Anonymous

MARY HAD A LITTLE LAMB

(version two)

Mary had a little lamb,
A little pork,
A little jam,
A little soda topped with fizz.
Now how sick our Mary is.

More Folk and Fairy Tale Poems

"In Search of Cinderella," p. 162, in A LIGHT IN THE ATTIC by Shel Silverstein (Harper & Row, 1981).

"Fairy Tale Poems," pp. 28-32, in IF I WERE IN CHARGE OF THE WORLD by Judith Viorst, il. by Lynne Cherry (Atheneum, 1981).

"The Gingerbread Man," p. 50, in SING A SONG OF POPCORN, poems selected by Beatrice Schenk de Regniers, Eva Moore, Mary Michaels White, and Jan Carr (Scholastic, 1988).

OLD MACDONALD HAD A FOLK TALE

(Suit actions to words.)
Old MacDonald had a folk tale,
E-I-E-I-O!
And in this tale was Little Red Riding Hood,
E-I-E-I-O!
With a walk, walk here and a walk, walk
    there,
Here a walk, there a walk,
Everywhere a walk, walk,
Old MacDonald had a folk tale,
E-I-E-I-O!

Additional verses: Tale: Gingerbread man (run, run), Jack and the Beanstalk (climb, climb), Greedy Old Fat Man (eat, eat). Let the children create their own verses. It's best to sing only 3 or 4 verses at a time so the children won't tire of it.

CINDERELLA DRESSED IN "YELLA"

(jump rope jingle)
Cinderella dressed in "yella"
Went upstairs to kiss her fella.
By mistake, she kissed a snake.
How many doctors did it take?
One, two, three, four, five . . .
—Anonymous

More Folk and Fairy Tale Songs

"Who's Afraid of the Big Bad Wolf?," p. 52 and "Whistle While You Work," p. 62, in READER'S DIGEST CHILDREN'S SONG BOOK (Reader's Digest General Books, 1985).

JIM ALONG, JOSIE, A COLLECTION OF FOLK SONGS, compiled by Nancy & John Lanstaff, il. by Jan Pienkowski (Harcourt Brace, 1970).

Other possibilities: "The Old Gray Mare," "Pop Goes the Weasel," "Shoo Fly," "Daisy Bell," and "On Top of Old Smokey."

⚞ Folk and Fairy Tale Dramatic Play ⚟

GREEDY OLD FAT MAN

Props: lightweight blanket, chair

Characters: man, little girl and boy, cat, dog, fox, several rabbits, squirrel

After reading the tale, assist the children in the dramatization. Choose characters. If not too large of a group, all of the children can participate (extra kids can be rabbits). Place the old man on a chair. Have someone drape a blanket around his or her chest and hold it together in the back. Tell the story while encouraging the characters to say their own dialogue. As the greedy old man "eats" them, the characters go under the blanket. When the squirrel tricks the old man, all come out and run away. Encourage the children to do the dramatization without adult assistance.

GINGERBREAD MAN

This story may be dramatized at the same time as it's being told. Each time the gingerbread man and the other characters run, have the children run in place. Use lots of facial expression as you read and ask the children to make the expressions along with you. When the gingerbread man is running away, keep turning your head to look back. Lift your legs high to pretend you're the gingerbread man climbing onto the fox's back. When the gingerbread man has been eaten, drop to the floor.

THE TURNIP

Props: gigantic turnip (refer to Folk and Fairy Tale Crafts)

Characters: Dedoushka, Baboushka, Mashenka, Geouchka, Keska, mouse

Choose characters. Also select someone to hold the turnip. Then tell the tale as the children act it out and say their own dialogue. Encourage the children to holler out when calling for help. They will love saying the Russian names. A word of caution: the children must be careful when they fall down as the turnip comes out of the ground so they don't land on top of each other and get hurt. Dramatize the tale as many times as necessary to give each child the opportunity to be an actor.

Folk and Fairy Tale Crafts

PEA ON A PILLOW

Materials: dried peas, fabric, cotton, glue, stapler

Directions: Provide each child with two small squares of fabric. Let the children staple or glue three sides together and wait for the squares to dry. Have the children stuff their "pillow" with cotton and then staple or glue the fourth side closed. When the pillow is dry, children can glue a dried pea to the top of the pillow. Encourage children to use this prop when retelling the tale of the PRINCESS AND THE PEA.

KETTLEDRUM

Materials: round oatmeal box or large can with top cut out, heavy fabric, rubber band, scissors

Directions: Help each child cut a round piece of fabric to fit over the top of the box. Show them how to hold it in place with a rubber band. Let the children play their drums using both hands, experimenting with different rhythms. Make this craft in conjunction with the reading of RUM PUM PUM.

MITTEN

Materials: 2 yards yellow fur-type fabric, 2 yards red flannel, 1/2 yard white fuzzy-type fabric, 3 1/2 yards Velcro, sewing supplies, mitten pattern, forest creature patterns

Directions: Fold the yellow fabric in half and cut out a mitten shape the size of the fabric. Use the mitten as a pattern to cut two pieces of red flannel. Put the right sides of each flannel and yellow fabric piece together and stitch together around the edges, leaving a small opening. Pull the fabric right-side out through the opening. Stitch opening closed. Sew Velcro around the edges of the flannel. Press the two pieces together to make the mitten. To make the cuff, cut a strip of white fuzzy fabric the width of the top of the mitten, about 18" wide. Fold over to make the cuff 9" wide and sew to the top of the mitten.

When finished, stuff the mitten with forest creatures. Refer to the Read-Aloud section for ways to use this prop after reading THE MITTEN.

GIGANTIC TURNIP

Materials: white and green paper, scissors, stapler, old newspaper, purple chalk or paint

Directions: Ahead of time, cut out two large turnip shapes (about 2' X 3') from white paper and one stem from green paper for every three children in your classroom. Staple three sides of the turnip pieces together leaving one side open for stuffing. Let the children use purple chalk or paint to color the upper part of the turnip, then crumple newspaper and stuff the turnip. Staple the open edges together and staple a stem onto each turnip. Divide the children into groups of three or four and give each group a turnip. The children will enjoy using this prop to dramatize THE TURNIP. Place the turnips in the dramatic play corner as a reminder of the fabulous tale.

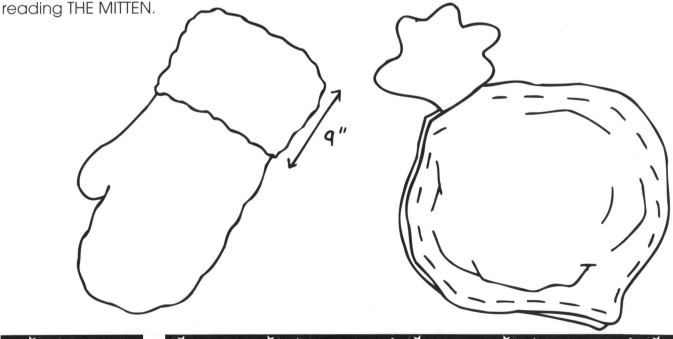

Mitten Pattern

Staple.

Staple.

Staple.

58

Forest Creature Patterns

LITTLE RED HEN'S BREAD

Use a simple bread recipe to make bread. Let the children help as much as possible. (You may want to ask for some parent volunteers to help.) Dramatize the story as you're making the bread. Provide some wheat (available at health food stores) and a mortar and pestle for children to try grinding wheat into flour.

GINGERBREAD MAN

Make a favorite gingerbread cookie recipe, or follow the directions on a box of prepared gingerbread mix for making cookies. Use the pattern provided to make one or more large gingerbread men. Trim with frosting. Add raisin eyes. After reading the tale, explain that you're the sly fox who caught the gingerbread man, but you would like to share him with the children. Let the children pretend they're foxes. Serve the gingerbread man with milk.

RUNAWAY PANCAKES

Make a batch of pancakes from your favorite pancake mix. But don't let them run away! Eat them instead. Make a face on the pancakes using raisins or nuts. Invite parents to share a special breakfast treat with the students.

POP GHOSTS

ball-shaped lollipops
white cocktail-size napkins
black marker
yarn

To make the ghosts, wrap one napkin around each lollipop and tie with yarn. Draw big ghost eyes with a marker and give the scary treats to the children. Great for Halloween!

RUMPELSTILTSKINS
(2 servings)

baked potato
2 teaspoons finely chopped cooked
   bacon
2 teaspoons shredded Cheddar cheese
butter

Slice the potato into two pieces lengthwise and scoop out the potato leaving about a 1/4" shell. Place in a baking dish. Spread with butter, bacon, and Cheddar cheese, and bake in a 350 degree oven for about 5 minutes.

There is magic in books! Tomie de Paola has written several books about Strega Nona, a friendly witch who performs silly magic. A sampling of de Paola's books are listed in this chapter, and it might be fun to hold a special Tomie de Paola week and read only his books.

Teach the children some magic words—"Abracadabra Alakazaam," "Hocus Pocus," and "Presto" are a few good choices. Have the children open and close their hands while saying these words—they might even want to close their eyes to make the magic work better.

For something very special, show the children how to turn stones into books. Give each child a magic stone. When the child drops it into a bag (filled with books), give the child a book to borrow.

Visit a magic shop to gather additional ideas.

SETTING THE STAGE

Paint or cover a box with black paper. Enlarge the magic hat pattern (see Magic Crafts) and attach it to the box. Store magic-theme books in the magic hat box. You can also make a wearable magic hat from heavy paper.

Decorate the walls of the room with black hats, magic wands, white rabbits, tissue paper flowers, and fairy dust (glitter) to create a delightful and magical atmosphere.

Make fairy wings for the children to wear during dramatic play (see Magic Crafts).

Attach book titles to scarves and place them in a black hat. When it's story time, let the children take turns pulling out a title of a story to be read. Place a magic carpet (piece of carpet or blanket) on the floor in the reading center for the children to sit on while reading books about magic.

BULLETIN BOARD IDEAS

1. Enlarge, color, and cut out the "Books Are Magic" illustration. To perform a little magic, cut out the hat and book separately and attach a tab to the book to raise it in and out of the hat.

2. Copy a picture of Tomie de Paola from the inside cover of one of his books. Pin up the picture with copies of covers from some of his books. Also include a short biography listing his accomplishments.

3. Make Amanda's gigantic vegetables after reading AMANDA AND THE MAGIC GARDEN by John Himmelman. The children will enjoy cooperating to make these, perhaps in groups of three or four.

Books Are Magic

CAT AND ALEX AND THE MAGIC FLYING CARPET
by Robin Ballard (HarperCollins, 1991).

Story: Cat visits his friend Alex, a small boy, and together they enjoy a cup of hot cocoa while sitting by the fireplace. Cat relates his adventures on his magic carpet and then invites Alex to go along with him on his next adventure.

Materials: magic carpets (carpet samples, large blankets, or rugs)

Directions: In a quiet, darkened room, provide magic carpets for the children to sit on while listening to this story. Ask the children to lie down on their carpets, close their eyes, and pretend to visit the moon with Cat and Alex. Then encourage the children to embark upon their own adventures. After their travels, the children might enjoy sharing their adventures with each other. For a special treat, serve cocoa or tea and coconut cookies.

FAT MAGIC
by Steven Kroll, il. by Tomie de Paola (Holiday House, 1978).

Story: Prince Timothy spends all of his time eating or thinking about ice cream sundaes, pies, and cakes. One day, Edgar, the court magician, casts a spell on Prince Timothy that makes him very, very fat. But Prince Timothy learns the secret to Edgar's magic (Edgar's shoes), and puts an end to all the teasing about his love of food.

Materials: bowl of cereal, bowl of jelly beans, magic hat (see Magic Crafts), shoes, orange felt

Directions: Cover the top of a regular pair of shoes with orange felt to look similar to those in the story. After reading the book, put on the shoes and the magic hat. Bring out a bowl of cereal and explain that because you're wearing magic shoes, you can change the cereal into jelly beans. Ask the children to close their eyes, repeat some magic words, and exchange the cereal for jelly beans. When the children open their eyes they'll see a bowl of jelly beans. Invite them to share the treat.

THE MAGIC FAN
by Keith Baker (Harcourt Brace, 1989).

Story: In a village by the sea, a young boy named Yoshi builds everything the people need. One night, a magic fan floats in from the sea and Yoshi follows it. He builds a boat to catch the moon, a kite to reach the sky, and a bridge that saves the village people from a tsunami.

Materials: various fans, magic fan pattern (see Magic Crafts), markers

Directions: Collect an assortment of fans to display in the classroom. Introduce this story by showing the children a fan and talking about its uses. Then ask if it's a magic fan and, if so, what kind of magic it can perform. Does it have a functionary use? Remind children that some fans are delicate and must be handled carefully. Use the pattern provided for the children to make magic fans. Encourage them to decorate the fans with their own designs.

THE MAGIC WINGS
(A Tale from China)
by Diane Wolkstein, il. by Robert Andrew Parker (Unicorn, 1983).

Story: On a spring day in a flower-filled meadow, a little Chinese goose girl sprinkles water on her shoulders, waves her arms, and sprouts wings. Soon every woman in town, including the Queen and Princesses, are waving their arms so they might fly also. But only the Spirit in Heaven Who Grows Wings decides who shall have wings.

Materials: spring flowers

Directions: Introduce this folk tale by showing the children a variety of spring flowers. (If you tell this story during the spring, you can take the children on a nature walk to look at flowers.) Discuss the names of the flowers. Give each child a flower to take home. This will encourage the children to retell the story to other people. It is more effective to tell this story rather than read it because your arms will be free for dramatization. Refer to the Magic Tricks and Dramatic Play section for additional ideas.

STREGA NONA

retold and il. by Tomie de Paola
(Prentice-Hall, 1975).

Story: Strega Nona's magic pasta pot cooks pasta when she sings a magical chant. Big Anthony discovers her magic secret and cooks up a huge pot of pasta. Unfortunately, he doesn't know how to turn the pot off! The village is overrun with pasta before Strega Nona returns to use her magical powers to stop the magic pasta pot.

Materials: black pot, cooked pasta, forks and paper plates, modeling clay

Directions: Ahead of time, prepare pasta. Put the pasta in a container and fit it inside a black, magic pot. As you read the story, ask the children to join in on the singing of the magical chants. Then perform some magic of your own! Repeat the magical chants over the pot, then use a fork to make the pasta magically appear and serve it to everyone. Provide modeling clay for the children to make their own magic pots. What kind of magic will they perform?

SYLVESTER AND THE MAGIC PEBBLE

by William Steig (Prentice-Hall, 1969).

Story: Sylvester the donkey uses his magic pebble to turn himself into a huge rock, but then he's not able to hold the pebble to wish himself back to his natural form. When his parents are on a picnic some time later, they unknowingly pick up the pebble and wish their son alive again. The three live happily ever after.

Materials: magic red pebble and regular pebbles, red paint, paintbrushes

Directions: Show the children several pebbles along with the magic pebble that's been painted red. Pick out the red pebble and explain that it's magic. Read the story, paraphrasing for younger children. Then let the children paint the remaining pebbles red so they each have a magic pebble.

Alexander, Martha. **MY OUTRAGEOUS FRIEND CHARLIE** (Dial, 1989).

Jessie Mae admires her outrageous friend Charlie who can walk on stilts and dive from the high dive—wow! But when Charlie gives Jessie Mae a Super Deluxe Triple Magic Kit for her birthday, she discovers she can perform magic, and be just as outrageous as Charlie.

Alison, Lester. **MAGIC BEACH** (Joy Street/Little, 1992).

In this rhyming tale, a child's ordinary activities at the beach turn into imaginative adventures. Splashing waves become white, wild horses, a sand castle becomes the scene of an heroic rescue. And while searching for seashells the child discovers a chest of glistening treasures.

Banks, Kate, il. by Peter Sis. **ALPHABET SOUP** (Knopf, 1988).

A young boy spells "Bear" with his alphabet soup and magically a friendly bear appears. Together they go on a journey. Along the way, the boy spells the names of objects that come alive and help the two in their travels. When the journey ends, the boy has eaten all of his soup.

Brisson, Pat, il. by Amy Schwartz. **MAGIC CARPET** (Bradbury, 1991).

Elizabeth and Aunt Agatha imagine how an Oriental carpet might have traveled to their house from China. They make up characters and stories as they themselves travel through Japan to Anchorage.

Cartwright, Ann, il. by Reg Cartright. **POLLY AND THE PRIVET BIRD** (Hutchinson, 1992).

Polly trims an untidy privet bush into the shape of a bird, and the bush comes alive! The grown-ups are blind to the bird's magic when Polly and the bird rescue some children and help the townspeople survive a flood.

Christelow, Eileen. **OLIVE AND THE MAGIC HAT** (Clarion, 1987).

Playing with their father's tall black hat (which is to be his birthday present), Olive and Otis Opossum accidentally discover its magical powers.

Cole, Joanna, il. by Donald Carrick. **DOCTOR CHANGE** (William Morrow, 1986).

Based on a traditional folk tale theme, a young boy named Tom is trapped in the service of a magician, Doctor Change, who in an instant can change himself into a cat, a dog, or a pair of shoes. Tom learns his master's secrets and soon outwits him.

Cole, Joanna, il. by True Kelley. **MIXED-UP MAGIC** (Scholastic, 1987).

Maggie finds a little elf magician in her garden who agrees to grant her wishes. However, the elf's magic is mixed up and when he wishes for a coat he gets a boat, a goat, and a moat. The problem is solved when Maggie wishes for a float . . . and gets a coat!

Delton, Judy, il. by Bruce Degen. **BRIMHALL TURNS TO MAGIC** (Lothrop, Lee & Shepard, 1979).

Brimhall the bear decides he wants to become a magician. He gathers up his magic hat, his magic wand, and his magic cape. But when he pulls a rabbit out of the hat, Brimhall can't get the rabbit to go back in.

De Paola, Tomie. **BIG ANTHONY AND THE MAGIC RING** (Harcourt Brace, 1979).

Strega Nona (Grandma Witch) convinces Big Anthony he needs a little night life to get himself out of the doldrums. But Big Anthony doesn't want to go until he uses Strega Nona's magic ring to turn him into a handsome prince. Unfortunately, he gets into more trouble than he has fun.

De Paola, Tomie. **STREGA NONA'S MAGIC LESSONS** (Harcourt Brace, 1982).

Bambolona, the baker's daughter, must do all the baking while her father "loafs" around all day with his friends. She becomes disgusted and goes off to see Strega Nona to learn magic. Big Anthony wants to learn magic also, so he disguises himself as a girl. The two take magic lessons from Strega Nona.

Forest, Heather, il. by Susan Gaber. **THE WOMAN WHO FLUMMOXED THE FAIRIES** (Harcourt Brace, 1988).

The fairies capture the baker woman so she will bake them her finest cakes. Magically, the ground opens and the fairies return to the baker woman's house to retrieve the cake ingredients, but the baker woman flummoxes (befuddles) the fairies. All ends well when the baker woman returns home and agrees to leave cakes on the hill for the fairies to eat.

Fox, Mem, il. by Julie Vivas. **POSSUM MAGIC** (Abingdon, 1987).

Grandma Poss and Hush are two possums living in Australia. Grandma Poss can perform wonderful magic, but when she makes Hush invisible, she can't find a way to make him visible again. The two possums travel throughout Australia eating various foods in search of the magic cure that will make Hush visible again.

Gackenbach, Dick. **MAG THE MAGNIFICENT** (Clarion, 1985).

A little boy draws the magical monster Mag on the wall. Mag then jumps off the wall and goes with the boy on a series of magical adventures that last until the boy's mother asks him to clean the wall. However, the boy finds another way to save his magical monster.

Ginsburg, Mirra, il. by Linda Heller. **THE MAGIC STOVE** (Coward-McCann, 1983).

A poor old man and his wife own nothing but a rooster who finds a magic stove that makes delicious pies. The couple is very happy until the king steals the magic stove for his own use, but the clever rooster tricks the king and returns the stove to the old couple.

Graham, Bob. **GRANDAD'S MAGIC** (Little, Brown, 1989).

Alison loves her grandad's magic so much that she decides to learn a trick herself—juggling the sand-filled puffins. Grandad is jealous of her success and attempts to whip off the tablecloth from under Sunday lunch, but it's disastrous.

Haviland, Virginia, il. by Melissa Sweet. **THE TALKING POT** (Little, Brown, 1990).

This Danish folk tale, retold especially for young children, concerns a poor farmer who trades his last possession, a cow, for a talking pot. The pot skips off to a rich couple's house where it tricks them into filling it first with pudding, then flour, and eventually with gold coins. Thanks to the magical pot, the poor family lives happily ever after.

Hawkins, Colin and Jacqui. **MAX AND THE MAGIC WORD** (Viking Kestral, 1986).

Max, a dog, wants a piece of cake, to have a turn blowing bubbles, and to ride the tricycle. He doesn't get anything until he learns the magic word "please."

Himmelman, John. **AMANDA AND THE MAGIC GARDEN** (Viking Kestrel, 1987).

When Amanda plants magic seeds in her garden, the carrots grow as tall as buildings and the melons are mountainous. But when animals nibble on the vegetables they become gigantic, too. Amanda thinks of a counter spell and all ends well.

Houghton, Eric, il. by Denise Teasdale. **WALTER'S MAGIC WAND** (Orchard, 1989).

Walter takes his magic wand to the library where he taps a few exotic books and conjures up tigers, pirates, and even an ocean. This complicates the librarian's tidiness, but she seems to have an answer for every terror that Walter creates.

Karlin, Nurit. **THE TOOTH WITCH** (Lippincott, 1985).

The Tooth Witch flies over the world collecting the baby teeth that children lose. When she bungles the job, an apprentice is assigned to help her. The apprentice magically transforms into the very same Tooth Fairy that all little children know today.

Kellogg, Steven. **THE MYSTERY OF THE GREEN BALL** (Dial, 1978).

Timmy loses his cherished green ball while playing in the woods. He searches through the seasons, fall, winter, and spring, but can't find it. During a neighborhood carnival, Timmy discovers that

Sara, the neighborhood magician, is using it. He uses a little magic of his own to retrieve it.

Kent, Jack. **CLOTILDA'S MAGIC** (Scholastic, 1978).

Clotilda, a fairy godmother, feels sorry for herself when nobody shows interest in her magic. To gain their favor, Clotilda grants wishes for Tommy and Betty and finally grants Betty's wish for Clotilda to be her own personal fairy godmother.

Kopald, Suzanne Kelley. **SERINA'S FIRST FLIGHT: A TOOTH FAIRY'S TALE** (Thomasson-Gant, 1992).

When Serina makes her trial flight as a tooth fairy, she drops her silver coins in a dark pond. She needs the coins to exchange for baby teeth. A talking frog, an enchanted carp, and a rambunctious elf come to her aid and she successfully completes her first flight.

Kraus, Robert, il. by Mischa Richter. **BUNYA THE WITCH** (Simon & Schuster, 1971).

An old lady who lives on the edge of town discovers that she has magical powers. She turns all of the children into frogs and the parents into pigs. After the townspeople agree to be kind to her, things return to normal.

Lester, Helen, il. by Lynn Munsinger. **THE REVENGE OF THE MAGIC CHICKEN** (Houghton Mifflin, 1990).

The magic chicken, the wizard, and the fairy are having their daily argument about who is the greatest in the world. Finally, the magic chicken attempts revenge on his friends, and an enormous mess is created when his magic gets out of control.

Lester, Helen, il. by Lynn Munsinger. **THE WIZARD, THE FAIRY AND THE MAGIC CHICKEN** (Houghton Mifflin, 1983).

Three boastful magicians—a wizard, a fairy, and a chicken—try to outdo one another. When their magic creates three angry monsters, the magicians must learn to work together to solve their problem.

Littledale, Freya, il. by Winslow Pinney Pels. **THE MAGIC FISH** (Scholastic, 1985).

In this folk fairy tale, a fisherman catches a magic fish but returns it to the water in an act of kindness. His greedy wife makes him go back to the sea to ask the fish to grant her many wishes. The fish agrees until the wife becomes too greedy and he takes away all of her riches.

McAllister, Angela, il. by Margaret Chamberlain. **THE ENCHANTED FLUTE** (Delacorte, 1990).

Queen Persnickety is fussy. She demands that her subjects find the most amazing, most spectacular flute in the world for her daughter's birthday. The flute they find has magical powers and goes to work putting the fussbudget queen in her proper place.

McDermott, Gerald. **TIM O'TOOLE AND THE WEE FOLK** (Viking, 1990).

Tim O'Toole and his wife are so poor that they haven't a crumb to eat. Luckily, Tim discovers some wee folk who give him a magic goose and tablecloth that will provide golden eggs and food for the family forever. The horrible McGoon family attempts to steal the possessions, but again the wee folk come to the rescue of the O'Tooles.

McPhail, David. **THE MAGICAL DRAWINGS OF MOONEY B. FINCH** (Doubleday, 1978).

Mooney B. Finch is a young, talented artist who can draw just about anything. Then one day he discovers his drawings are magical—they slip off the drawing paper and become alive. When people become greedy and want Mooney to make valuables materialize, he teaches them a lesson by drawing a dragon that chases them away.

McPhail, David. **PIG PIG AND THE MAGIC PHOTO ALBUM** (Dutton, 1986).

Pig Pig looks at a magic photo album while waiting for the photographer to take his picture. Each time Pig Pig says "cheese" he magically appears in the photo he's looking at. After several adventures, he decides he wants his photo taken without saying "cheese."

Meyers, Odette, il. by Margot Zemach. **THE ENCHANTED UMBRELLA** (Gulliver, 1988).

Young Patou's magical umbrella lifts him into the air to escape from danger. Patou lands on a faraway shore where the people crown him their king. He's very happy living there and teaches all the people how to make umbrellas.

Moss, Marissa. **BUT NOT KATE** (Lothrop, Lee & Shepard, 1992).

Kate, a little mouse, doesn't feel that she's special in any way until she's chosen to assist the magician at the school magic show. Kate makes flowers appear and pulls rabbits out of a hat. When she discovers she does have some unique talents, she feels great about herself.

⭐ Magic Poems and Action Verses ⭐

MOON, MOON SO ROUND IN THE SKY

Moon, moon, so round in the sky,
How did you get up there?
Did someone toss you in the air?
Sun, sun, so bright in the sky,
Where did you get your light?
It's magic how you shine so bright!

MAGICAL SKY

It's magic how the stars appear
When the lights go out.
Where do all those stars come from?
What are they all about?
I love to watch those gleaming stars,
Twinkling in the sky.
I love to see their lovely light,
Shining from oh, so high.

THERE WERE TWO BLACKBIRDS

(Watch the blackbirds magically appear and disappear.)

There were two blackbirds,
Sitting on a hill. (Place index fingers on
   shoulders.)
One was named Jack. (Bring one finger
   off shoulder.)
The other named Jill. (Bring the other
   finger off shoulder.)
Fly away, Jack! (Put finger behind
   shoulder.)
Fly away, Jill! (Put other finger behind
   shoulder.)
Come back again, Jack! (Bring finger
   back.)
Come back again, Jill! (Bring other
   finger back.)

THE MAGIC WIND

The wind is magical today. (Blow lightly.)
It blew my brand new hat away. (Move
arm in tumbling motion.)
It chased my paper down the street,
(Run in place.)
And nearly blew me off my feet.
(Pretend you're nearly falling.)
It made the trees bend way down low,
(Bend at the waist.)
And swing and dance both to and fro.
(With arms up sway and dance.)

More Magic Poems and Action Verses

"Ten Fingers," pp. 34-35, in LISTEN! AND HELP TELL THE STORY by Bernice Carlson, il. by Burmak Burris (Abingdon, 1965).

"Puddle Magic," p. 73, in RING A RING O'ROSES (Flint Public Library, 1988).

"Maytime Magic," p. 44, "Thanksgiving Magic," p. 46, and "The Library," p. 220, in THE RANDOM HOUSE BOOK OF POETRY FOR CHILDREN selected by Jack Prelutsky, il. by Marc Brown (Random House, 1983).

"Magic," p. 11 and "Magical Eraser," p. 99, in WHERE THE SIDEWALK ENDS by Shel Silverstein (Harper & Row, 1974).

"Magic Carpet," p. 20, in A LIGHT IN THE ATTIC by Shel Silverstein (Harper and Row, 1981).

THE MAGIC FISH
(Tune: "Down by the Station")

The children will especially enjoy singing this song after reading THE MAGIC FISH.

Down by the ocean, early in the
  morning.
See the kindly fisherman catch the
  magic fish.
See the little, sad wife wish for all the
  riches.
"No, no! No, no!" says the fish.

WHERE IS THUMBKIN?
(Tune: "Are You Sleeping?")

The different fingers "magically" appear as they come from behind your back.

Where is Thumbkin? Where is Thumbkin?
Here I am. Here I am. (Bring out thumbs
  from behind back one at a time.)
How are you today, sir? (Wiggle one
  thumb.)
Very well, I thank you. (Wiggle other
  thumb.)
Run away, run away. (Put thumbs
  behind back again.)
—Unknown

Continue with additional verses using the appropriate finger for each verse: Where is pointer? Where is middle? Where is ringer? Where is pinky?

THE MAGIC STOVE
(Tune: "The Bear Went Over the Mountain")

What a thief the king is,
What a thief the king is,
Oh, what a thief the king is,
He stole the magic stove.
He stole the magic stove.
He stole the magic stove.
The rooster chased the king,
The rooster chased the king,
The rooster chased the king,
To get the magic stove.
To get the magic stove,
To get the magic stove.
The rooster got it back,
The rooster got it back,
The rooster got it back,
He saved the magic stove.

⭐ Magic Tricks and Dramatic Play ⭐

MAGIC TRICKS

The children will enjoy performing these magic tricks while wearing a black magic hat (see Magic Crafts).

Magic Ball

Pretend to put a small ball in your mouth, puffing out your cheeks to show that the ball is there. Deflate your cheeks as you pull the ball out from your ear. Keep the ball in your hand the entire time.

Magic Egg

Give a raw egg a good swirl on a table. Explain that when you touch it, the egg will stop; when you lift your finger, it will begin to spin again. It's a magic egg!

Magic Paper Tube

Prepare two magic tubes by rolling up sheets of heavy paper and taping the edges together. In one tube, insert clay into one end. Ask a child to hold the tube without clay upright on the table while you hold the tube with the clay in its end, clay end down. When you both lift your hands off the tubes, the child's will fall while your tube will remain standing. Say some magic words before you lift your hand off your tube!

THE MAGIC WINGS

This story (see page 64) lends itself to dramatization. As you tell the story, playing the role of the Spirit Who Grows Wings, choose a girl to be the Goose Girl and have her start waving her arms, followed by the grocer's daughters, the judge's daughter, the princess, and the queen. Finally have all the children participate by being the girls and women. Or read the story to the children first and then let them dramatize it themselves with little or no guidance.

Magic Books

FUNNY MAGIC: EASY TRICKS FOR YOUNG MAGICIANS by Rose Wyler and Gerald Ames (Parents Magazine Press, 1972).

IT'S MAGIC by Robert Lopshire (Macmillan, 1969).

GIVE A MAGIC SHOW! by Burton and Rita Marks, il. by Don Madden (Lothrop, Lee & Shepard, 1977).

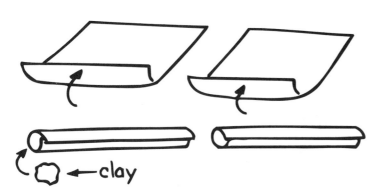

clay

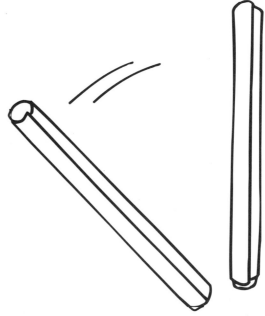

MAGIC BLACK HAT

Materials: hat patterns, black light-weight poster paper, stapler, scissors, glue, ruler

Directions: Provide hat patterns for each child. Help the children cut out the brim pattern on the fold. Show them how to unfold and cut out the brim, then cut out the top by centering the top pattern on the brim. Have them cut carefully. For each hat, cut an 8" X 20" strip, mark off a 1" line along the bottom and top, and cut through to the line at about 1/2" intervals. Fold the bottom tabs out and the top tabs in. Show the children how to bring the ends together to form a cylinder, overlapping the ends 1/2". Staple together. Let the children join the brim and the top to the hat tabs by gluing them together.

The hat size will fit a four- to five-year-old child; adjust the size for different ages. If desired, the children may make a hat band from black or any color of construction paper and glue it on. An elastic chin strap may be attached to hold the hat on better. When the hats are ready, have the children perform some marvelous magic!

WIZARD HAT

Materials: colored lightweight poster paper, hat pattern, scissors, stapler, glue, sparkles, markers

Directions: Double the size of the pattern provided; the curved brim should be about 24". Have each child color his or her hat with half-moon and star designs or spread with glue and sprinkle on sparkles. Help the children shape their hats into a cone shape and staple together. Use this craft in conjunction with the reading of FAT MAGIC or any book about wizards or magicians.

MAGIC FANS

Materials: fan pattern, Popsicle sticks, tape, colored markers or crayons, construction paper, scissors

Directions: Use the fan pattern provided to make one for each child. Let the children draw on designs similar to those in the story or create their own. Help the children tape a Popsicle stick to the back of their fan for a handle. They may use their fans for keeping cool on a hot day, for performing a little magic, or for retelling the story THE MAGIC FAN.

FAIRY WINGS

Materials: wing pattern, lightweight colored poster paper (blotter paper works well), ribbon, stapler, colored chalk, scissors, fix-it or hair spray

Directions: Enlarge the wing pattern onto poster paper and cut out two for each child. Cut two 20-inch pieces of ribbon for each child. If desired, let the children use various colors of chalk to shade the wings. Since chalk smears, spray it with fix-it or hair spray in an open area. Show the children how to staple the ribbon to the wings as illustrated, tie the ribbon in a bow, and slip the wings over their head. If you wish, make several sets of wings for the dress-up corner instead of one for each child.

WALTER'S MAGIC WAND

Materials: twig, glue, colored tissue paper, scissors

Directions: Have the children help gather twigs suitable for magic wands. Provide them with small pieces of different colors of tissue paper and have them glue the pieces to the twigs, wrapping them around as they glue. Let the children use their colorful wands in conjunction with the reading of WALTER'S MAGIC WAND, or any time they want to perform some magic.

Top Hat Pattern

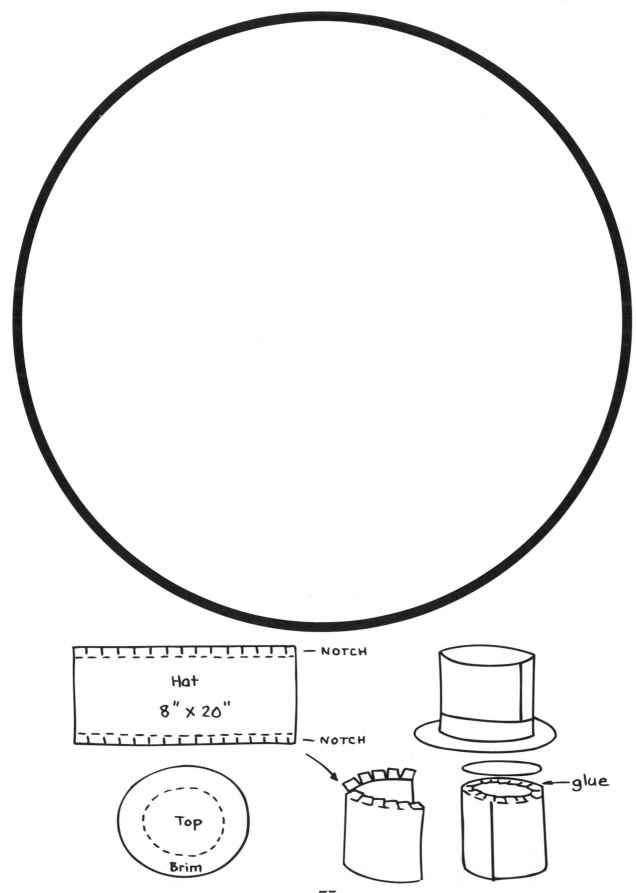

Hat
8" x 20"

— NOTCH

— NOTCH

Top

Brim

glue

Top Hat Pattern

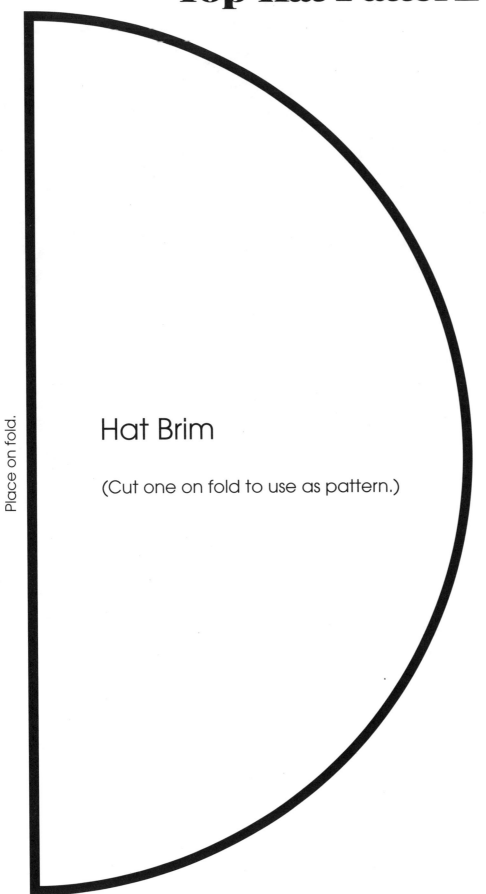

Place on fold.

Hat Brim

(Cut one on fold to use as pattern.)

Wizard Hat Pattern

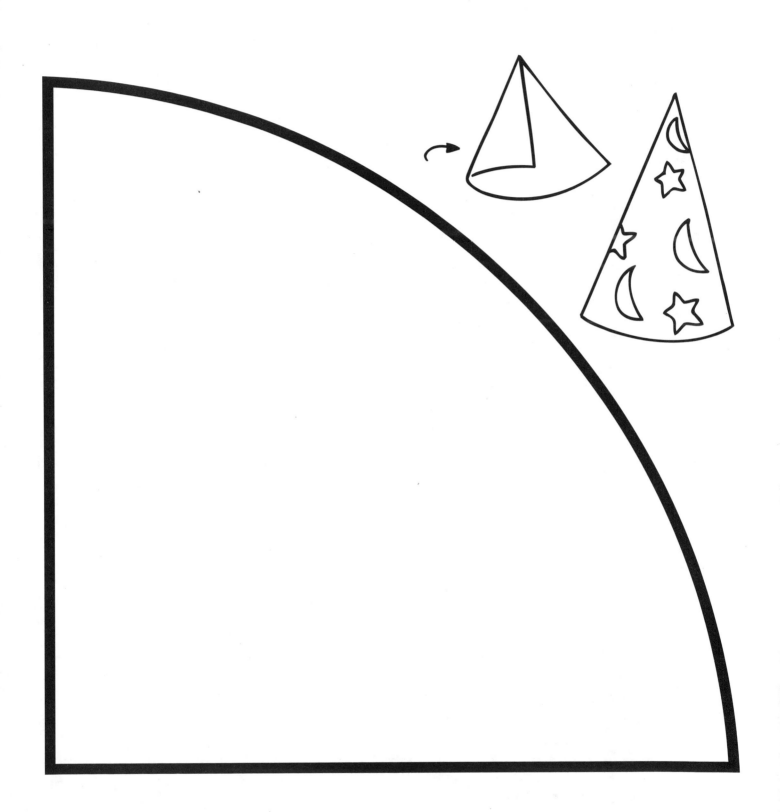

Fan Pattern

Wing Pattern

Staple ribbons here.

79

For a magical effect, cover any snack with a cloth and pull it off magician-style when you're ready to serve it.

MAGIC CARPET SANDWICHES

This is an easy snack children will love to make themselves!

bread slices
soft or whipped cream cheese
string licorice

Trim the crust off each slice of bread and cut the bread in two pieces to form two rectangular shapes (two carpets). Spread with cream cheese and place a string licorice piece on each to make stripes in the carpet.

MAGIC BANANAS

1 package strawberry-flavored gelatin
bananas (or any favorite fresh fruit)

Slice the bananas into a bowl. Sprinkle the dry gelatin over the bananas and watch the magic as they turn color!

MAGIC PICKLE WANDS

After reading THE REVENGE OF THE MAGIC CHICKEN by Helen Lester, the children will enjoy making their own magic wand by inserting a Popsicle stick into a pickle. After a little magic is performed, the eating begins.

Anything is possible in the world of make-believe, and books are the entry tickets. In a make-believe world, imagination lets us soar above trees on a warm summer day, talk with animals, and turn straw into gold. A reader can become a hero or a heroine, a fiery dragon, a friendly fish, a pretty flower, or even a cheese sandwich.

To enter the land of make-believe, have the children form a train, one behind another, each holding the waist of the child in front. Have the "train" go around the room making clickety-clack and choo-choo sounds. You should play the conductor. When you stop the train, inform the children that they have arrived in a magical land where they will be able to hear some merry make-believe stories.

SETTING THE STAGE

Create a room full of make-believe characters. Enlarge familiar characters from books, then color and cut them out to post around the room. Suspend lily pads with frogs from the ceiling. Also cut out big white clouds to suspend. Allow children to lie on their backs to observe the clouds overhead. Refer to Make-Believe Crafts for more suggestions. Display a stuffed version of Clifford, the big red dog, on a shelf, or put him in the reading corner for the children to rest their heads on while reading. Clifford is also available as a puppet. Display Clifford books nearby. Find a big, sturdy dresser drawer to set on the floor for the children to sit in while reading books. Throw in a few socks to make it look like the drawer in THE BOY IN THE DRAWER by Robert Munsch.

BULLETIN BOARD IDEAS

1. Enlarge the illustration "Fly Away with A Book." Use pastels to color the background and bright primary colors for the flying child.

2. Cover a bulletin board with blue paper. Give the children white paper and scissors and ask them to each cut out a cloud. Pin up the clouds. Ask the children what each cloud shape looks like. Read IT LOOKED LIKE SPILT MILK by Charlie G. Shaw as a lead-in to this activity.

3. Enlarge an illustration of Clifford onto red paper. Draw on features, then cut out and glue on a collar, or use a real collar for a special effect.

4. Enlarge the beast in THE BEAST IN THE BATHTUB by Kathleen Stevens onto poster paper. Cut out. Use this pattern to cut out a beast from furry green fabric. Glue on features. Pin up as is or make a bathtub for the beast from poster paper.

5. Enlarge the cover of THE DARK by Robert Munsch. Color in the background. Make the "dark" three-dimensional by cutting out a second "dark," coloring and gluing it to the background with small pieces of foam rubber to make it stand out slightly.

Fly Away With a Book!

THE ADVENTURES OF ISABEL

by Ogden Nash, il. by James Marshall (Little, Brown, 1991).

Story: The feisty, inimitable Isabel eats a bear, turns a witch into milk, defeats a giant, gives the doctor a shot, and gets rid of a bugaboo.

Materials: bugaboo costume (see below), moveable Isabel cutout (see Make-Believe Crafts)

Directions: While reading, have the children join in on the refrain "Isabel, Isabel, didn't worry, Isabel didn't scream or scurry." Provide them with a moveable cutout to use as a prop when retelling the story. A simple bugaboo costume can be made by covering someone with a blanket or sheet and adding the features illustrated in the story. After reading the story, the bug-aboo can make an appearance to say "Boo!" to the children, and they can answer, "And boo to you!" Children are delighted when a character from a story comes alive.

THE BABY WHO WOULD NOT COME DOWN

by Joan Knight, il. by Debrah Santini (Picture Book Studio, 1989).

Story: The baby is tired of being tickled, bounced, and smothered in kisses, so when Uncle tosses him into the air he floats out the window and doesn't come down. When the family decides to mend its ways, the baby returns to give everybody a second chance.

Materials: toy baby doll or poster paper cutout, string

Directions: Beforehand, suspend a baby doll from the ceiling as if it's floating in the air. Just before reading the story, draw the children's attention to the doll and ask them why they think it might be up there. Leave the doll in the air as a reminder of the story and to intrigue guests who visit your classroom.

THE BOY IN THE DRAWER

by Robert Munsch, il. by Michael Martchenko (Annick, 1986).

Story: Shelley finds a little boy sitting in her sock drawer reading a book. Later, the boy paints her window black so she can't see out and takes a bath in the bread box. With the help of her parents, Shelley finally makes the troublesome little boy disappear.

Materials: dresser drawer, a few socks

Directions: Display the drawer with a few socks in it and talk about what might be in the drawer besides the socks. Finally, ask if it might be fun to sit in the drawer to listen to a book. Read the book and invite the children to take turns sitting in the drawer while listening.

BRUSH

by Pere Calders, il. by Carme Sole Vendell (Kane/Miller, 1988).

Story: Turco Sala's pet dog is banished from the house when it becomes too mischievous. Turco searches for another pet and finally adopts a large brush, which surprises him by coming alive and capturing a burglar. The entire family accepts the brush as a hero.

Materials: large brush with string attached, other inanimate objects

Directions: Show the brush to the children. Let them pet it and put it on the floor. Pull the string to make the brush move as if it is alive. Provide other objects that can be used as inanimate pets, for example, a sponge, rock, box, ball, pebble, ruler. Ask if any of the children have inanimate objects for pets, and encourage them to bring these "pets" for show and tell. If children think that you're kidding, tell them about the Pet Rock craze of the '70s—be prepared for lots of laughs!

THE DANCING SKELETON
by Cynthia C. DeFelice, il. by Robert Andrew Parker (Macmillan, 1989).

Story: An ornery man named Aaron Kelly is dead, but he refuses to stay in his coffin. He returns to his widow's home and rocks back and forth in his rocking chair until he becomes a skeleton. The best fiddler in town calls on the widow, but is frightened away when the skeleton begins to dance to his fiddle music.

Materials: skeleton pattern (see Make-Believe Crafts), fiddle music

Directions: Play a record of fast fiddle music, and make your skeleton dance to pieces! Refer to Make-Believe Games and Dramatic Play for additional ideas concerning this story.

THE DARK
by Robert N. Munsch, il. by Sami Suomalainen (Annick, 1988).

Story: Jule Ann turns the cookie jar upside down to find cookies, but instead a dark glob falls out and bounces across the table. It's a "dark," and it grows bigger and bigger as it eats shadows. Because it's so big, it becomes a nuisance, so Jule Ann uses shadows to trick the dark back inside the cookie jar.

Materials: big jar, black paper, black felt, scissors, tape, modeling clay

Directions: Ahead of time, make a cookie jar by covering a big glass jar with black paper. Cut out odd shapes of black felt or paper to represent pieces of shadows. Place them in the cookie jar. Read the story, encouraging the children to help by making the various sounds and repeating the phrases written in bold print. At the end of the story, bring out the cookie jar and let each child have a piece of shadow.

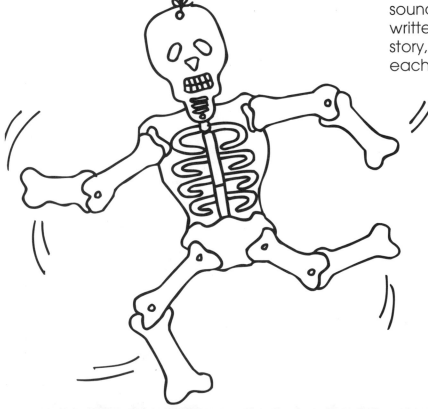

FRITZ AND THE MESS FAIRY
by Rosemary Wells (Dial, 1991).

Story: Fritz, a young badger, is a master at creating terrible messes around the house. One night as Fritz is sleeping, he dreams his science project turns into the Mess Fairy, who makes the biggest messes ever. Fritz finally decides it's time for him to change, and he begins to tidy up.

Materials: a stuffed badger in a striped tie or an enlarged cutout of Fritz, Mess Fairy puppets (see Make-Believe Crafts), lemonade, muffins, pink fabric, pipe cleaners, pink paper wings, star wand, jar of rose-colored water, paper, scissors

Directions: After reading the story, bring out the Mess Fairy puppet and Fritz. Hold a conversation between the two. Make a Mess Fairy costume with pink fabric, pipe cleaner antennae, wings, and a star wand. Set a jar filled with "rose water" (water dyed with food coloring) on a shelf or table. While children pretend to sleep, have the Mess Fairy begin to make a mess by throwing around some crinkled paper. It won't be too messy, but it will delight the children. Serve muffins and lemonade for a special treat. Refer to Make-Believe Snacks for a muffin recipe.

IMOGENE'S ANTLERS
by David Small (Crown, 1985).

Story: Imogene wakes up on Thursday morning and discovers that she has grown antlers. Her antlers are used as a bird feeder, candelabra, and clothesline. When her antler dilemma is finally solved, Imogene wakes up the following morning to discover that she has grown peacock feathers.

Materials: antler headbands (see Make-Believe Crafts)

Directions: Be quite dramatic when reading this story, and emphasize the mother's fainting spells. Let the children make antler headbands to use in dramatic play. Ask what they would do if they grew a set of antlers. If possible, have a carpenter make a set of plywood antlers, stabilized on a wood block, to place on a table. Let the children decorate the antlers with streamers or, for a special treat, serve them doughnuts or bagels on the antlers at snack time!

IT LOOKED LIKE SPILT MILK

by Charles G. Shaw (Harper & Row, 1988).

Story: Sometimes a cloud can look like spilt milk, an ice cream cone, a rabbit, a squirrel, or a birthday cake, but it's not. It's just a cloud high in the sky.

Materials: white paint, blue paper, straws

Directions: Be sure to show the illustrations to the children as you read this story. Encourage them to join in on the refrain "But it wasn't. . . ." As a group project, make a cloud mural on a sheet of rolled blue paper that's large enough for each child to paint a cloud. Spread the paper on the floor and pour a circle of white paint on it for each child. Have the children blow their paint through a straw to form a cloud. It's okay for the clouds to overlap. When dry, attach the mural to the ceiling. Have the children lie on the floor and imagine what the cloud shapes might be. Or read this book on a cloudy day and let the children lie on the grass outside to observe the clouds.

TUESDAY

by David Wiesner (Clarion, 1991). (Caldecott Winner, 1992)

Story: On Tuesday evening around eight o'clock, frogs levitate on their lily pads and float above the sleeping inhabitants. They float into living rooms and chase dogs. But when it's daylight, the only evidence of the frogs' visit are the lily pads strewn about town.

Materials: lily pads and frogs (see Make-Believe Crafts)

Directions: Because this is a wordless book, feel free to use any dialogue you wish. Be sure to study the illustrations carefully before presenting the story. Encourage the children to add their own ideas. Have each child hang his or her frog and lily pad around the room. Some frogs might be coming in the windows. Others might be watching from the bulletin board. Imagine what fun it will be to be in a room filled with floating frogs!

Alexander, Sue, il. by Chris L. Demarest. **WORLD FAMOUS MURIEL** (Little, Brown, 1984).

Muriel is a little girl who is famous for being a tightrope walker and a scholar. The queen invites Muriel to her birthday party to perform. When the decorative paper lanterns are missing from the party, the world famous Muriel solves the mystery before the party begins.

Allen, Pamela. **A LION IN THE NIGHT** (Puffin, 1988).

A baby makes a wish and rides away on a lion's back. Several people join in on the chase to rescue the baby. Eventually, the lion stops and roars at the chasers. But, because everyone's hungry after the long chase, the lion feeds them breakfast.

Baumann, Kurt, il. by Fulvio Testa. **THE PAPER AIRPLANE** (Little, Brown, 1981).

As a child flies his paper airplane out the window, he imagines he's flying with the birds over the ocean, above Africa, and into space. Directions are included for making a paper airplane.

Bradman, Tony, il. by Carol Wright. **IT CAME FROM OUTER SPACE** (Dial, 1992).

A spaceship crashes through the roof and lands in the classroom. An alien emerges who befriends the teacher and students. However, there is a surprise ending that will make everyone smile!

Bridwell, Norman. **CLIFFORD THE BIG RED DOG** (Scholastic, 1967).

Emily has the biggest, reddest dog on her street, and maybe in the world! Clifford lifts cars and policemen, takes a bath in the swimming pool, and gets his hair combed with a garden rake. Emily thinks that he's the best pet anyone could have. Other adventures about Clifford include CLIFFORD GOES TO HOLLYWOOD, CLIFFORD TAKES A TRIP, CLIFFORD'S HALLOWEEN, and CLIFFORD GETS A JOB.

Brown, M.K. **SALLY'S ROOM** (Scholastic, 1992).

One day after Sally leaves for school, the objects in her untidy room march down the street and burst into her class-room. There's a lamp shade festooned with dirty socks and a bed full of toys and puzzles. Sally hurries home and is impressed by all the space in her room. She decides that she will keep it clean in the future.

Burningham, John. **HEY! GET OFF THE TRAIN** (Crown, 1989).

At bedtime, a young boy and his dog board a toy train that takes them around the world. Along the way they encounter several endangered animals —an elephant, a polar bear, and several others. At first, the boy doesn't want them on his train, but when he learns the plight of each threatened animal he invites them aboard.

Burningham, John. **TIME TO GET OUT OF THE BATH, SHIRLEY** (Crowell, 1978).

Shirley's mother attempts to get her out of the bath and dry off, but Shirley is much too busy. She's jousting with knights, riding a beautiful horse, visiting an elaborate castle, and greeting kings and queens.

Christiana, David. **DRAWER IN A DRAWER** (Farrar, Straus & Giroux, 1990).

Fud is a drawer (or artist) who sits in a drawer and draws a line. The line turns into a box, and the box turns into a wild adventure that takes Fud up to the sky.

Here he takes a dip in the dipper before returning home to his drawer.

Cole, Babette. **THE TROUBLE WITH MOM** (Coward-McCann, 1983).

A young boy's mother isn't like other moms. When she doesn't agree with the parents at the P.T.A. meeting, she turns them into frogs, and her cupcakes contain bugs and frogs. However, when the school catches fire, Mom puts it out before the fire engines arrive, and everyone agrees Mom's talents do come in handy. Other zany books by Cole include THE TROUBLE WITH MY DAD and KING CHANGE-A-LOT.

Cooney, Nancy Evans, il. by Melissa Bay Mathis. **THE UMBRELLA DAY** (Philomel, 1989).

It's an "umbrella day," but Missy doesn't want to carry the big, old umbrella. When the rain does come, Missy and her umbrella enter an imaginative world where the umbrella turns into a toadstool, a circus tent, and a sailing boat.

Cooper, Susan, il. by Jos. A. Smith. **MATTHEW'S DRAGON** (McElderry, 1991).

The friendly miniature dragon in Matthew's picture book comes alive at bedtime. Matthew becomes the same size as the dragon, and the two pals embark on a great nocturnal adventure. They have an encounter with the neighbor's vicious cat, but escape by flying into the sky where every imaginable dragon is swirling around.

Davis, Douglas F., il. by Steven Kellogg. **THERE'S AN ELEPHANT IN THE GARAGE** (E. P. Dutton, 1979).

April Janice Jones and her cat Zelda run away to the garage where they hunt fierce animals. Zelda saves the day by capturing a rogue elephant who must stay in the garage until he learns some manners.

Faulkner, Matt. **THE AMAZING VOYAGE OF JACKIE GRACE** (Scholastic, 1987).

Young Jackie Grace is taking a bath when all of a sudden he finds himself in a ship headed for the high seas with a crew of sailors looking for their lost vessel. In their pursuit, Jackie becomes a hero until, just as suddenly, he finds himself back in his tub.

Fleischman, Paul, il. by Claire Ewart. **TIME TRAIN** (Zolotow, 1991).

A school class takes a trip on the Rocky Mountain Unlimited through prehistoric times to observe living dinosaurs. The children cook dinosaur eggs, go stegosaurus-back-riding, and glide with a pterodactyl before returning home.

Fox, Mem, il. by Vicky Kitanov. **ARABELLA, THE SMALLEST GIRL IN THE WORLD** (Scholastic, 1986).

Arabella is the smallest girl in the world. She has many ordinary possessions such as pillows, house plants, a bathtub, and a mirror. However, Arabella uses these possessions in delightfully different ways.

Goodspeed, Peter, il. by Dennis Panek. **A RHINOCEROS WAKES ME UP IN THE MORNING** (Bradbury, 1982).

A little boy's stuffed animals help him through the day. An elephant brushes the boy's teeth for him, a beaver grinds his oats, a unicorn takes him to school, and a walrus draws water for his bath.

Greenburg, Dan, il. by John Wallner. **THE BED WHO RAN AWAY FROM HOME** (HarperCollins, 1991).

Bosco Is a happy, carefree bunk bed until one night when the twins who sleep on his top and bottom come to bed late. The bunk bed feels abandoned and runs away from home. Bosco returns when he discovers that he's missed.

Harness, Cheryl. **THE WINDCHILD** (Holt, 1991).

Tom shoots an arrow up into the sky. When he goes to retrieve his arrow, he finds it is in the side of a sleeping girl named Windchild. The wind ceases to blow in the village of Finn until Windchild returns to the sky.

Heller, Nicholas. **THE TOOTH TREE** (Greenwillow, 1991).

Charlie doesn't believe in the Tooth Fairy so he buries his tooth in his treasure chest in the yard. Overnight, an odd-looking tooth tree grows and begins to eat everything in sight. Luckily, the Tooth Fairy appears and solves the problem.

Henrik, Drescher. **SIMON'S BOOK** (Lothrop, Lee & Shepard, 1983).

A young boy draws a story about Simon and the scary monster. While the boy sleeps, his characters come to life and finish the storybook.

Jensen, Helen. **WHEN PANDA CAME TO OUR HOUSE** (Dial, 1985).

A large, lovable panda comes from China to visit an American girl. The panda teaches the girl about China and they play and sing together. They become best friends.

Kirby, David and Allen Woodman, il. by Chris L. Demarest. **THE COWS ARE GOING TO PARIS** (Caroline House, 1991).

The cows decide to visit Paris in a horse-pulled carriage. They enjoy their trip, but when they return home, they decide it is just as satisfying to be there.

Kyoko, Matsuoka, il. by Akiko Hayashi. **THERE'S A HIPPO IN MY BATH** (Doubleday, 1982).

A young boy and his duck are enjoying their bath when they're joined by a sea turtle who pops his head out of the water. Then along come two penguins, a seal, a hippo, and a whale. However, when mother opens the door, all the animals disappear except for the duck.

Mahy, Margaret, il. by Helen Craig. **THE PUMPKIN MAN AND THE CRAFTY CREEPER** (Lothrop, Lee & Shepard, 1990).

Mr. Parkins, the pumpkin man, brings home a curious sprawling, talking vine. The vine demands to be entertained with music, dancing, and poetry. It drives Mr. Parkins crazy until Lily Rose Willowherb takes the Crafty Creeper home.

McPhail, David. **THE BEAR'S TOOTHACHE** (Little, Brown, 1972).

A bear with a toothache sits outside a young boy's bedroom. The boy invites him in and tries to pull the aching tooth. After much effort, the boy succeeds. As a reward, the bear gives the boy the tooth.

Munsch, Robert, il. by Giles Tibo. **GIANT** (Annick, 1989).

McKeon, the largest giant in all of Ireland, begins throwing church bells into the ocean when he becomes angry with St. Patrick for chasing away all the snakes, elves, and the other giants in Ireland. To get revenge, McKeon flies to heaven. He remains there today, throwing out church bells which we see as shooting stars.

Munsch, Robert, il. by Sami Suomalainen. **MUD PUDDLE** (Annick, 1982).

Every time Jule Ann walks outside in clean new clothes, a mud puddle jumps on her. Then she must take a bath. She tires of this routine, and tricks the mud puddle by throwing it bars of soap. The mud puddle never comes back.

Munsch, Robert, il. by Michael Martchenko. **MURMEL MURMEL MURMEL** (Annick, 1988).

Robin reaches into a hole in her sand-box and retrieves a baby sucking its pacifier. Because Robin is only five years old, she must find someone else to take care of the baby. She encounters several people, and finally finds a truck driver who wants the baby. He gives Robin his truck as a trade.

Munsch, Robert and Michael Kusugak, il. by Valdyana Krykorka. **A PROMISE IS A PROMISE** (Annick, 1988).

Allashua goes to the ocean to fish in the ice cracks. Her mother warns her that under the sea ice live Quallupilluit, imaginary Inuit creatures that look some-what like trolls. Allushua calls the Quallupilluit bad names, and when they appear she has a difficult time getting rid of them.

Oram, Hiawyn, il. by Satoshi Kitamura. **IN THE ATTIC** (Holt, Rinehart and Winston, 1984).

A child who is bored with all his toys imagines he climbs into the attic. There he and a spider build a web, the win-dows open onto other worlds, he makes friends with a talking tiger, and he flies in a flying machine.

Pinkwater, Daniel M., il. by James Marshall. **ROGER'S UMBRELLA** (Dutton, 1982).

Roger doesn't like his umbrella. It's wild and uncontrollable. Sometimes it lifts him several feet above the ground and carries him for blocks. At night it pops open and hops around his room. Then Roger meets three old ladies who teach him how to control the umbrella.

Rosenfeldt, Robert. **TIDDALICK, THE FROG WHO CAUSED A FLOOD** (Penguin, 1986).

A huge frog drinks all the water in Australia. There isn't any left for the other animals, who must come up with a plan to make the frog return the water.

Sadler, Marilyn, il. by Roger Bollen. **ALISTAIR'S TIME MACHINE** (Prentice-Hall, 1986).

Alistair's entry in the science compe-tition is a time machine. When he tests it out, he goes back to the time of the cave men and mammoths. Unfor-tunately, he can't prove it to the competition judges. Other books about Alistair include ALISTAIR'S ELEPHANT and ALISTAIR IN OUTER SPACE.

Samton, Shelia White. **JENNY'S JOURNEY** (Viking, 1991).

Jenny's best friend Maria writes her a letter saying that she is lonely. Jenny writes back right away and draws a picture of a sailboat. Jenny imagines she sails in it to visit Maria, who lives on a distant island.

Sherman, Nancy, il. by Edward Sorel. **GWENDOLYN THE MIRACLE HEN** (Golden Press, 1961).

This rhyme tells how Farmer Brown works from dawn to dusk in his fields, but still cannot make enough money to pay his rent to Mr. Meany, the landlord. Gwendolyn, the miracle hen, helps by laying beautiful multicolored eggs for the farmer to sell. To this very day, when the rent comes due, Gwendolyn's eggs appear.

Shoberg, Lore. **WILLY** (McGraw-Hill, 1974).

The class assignment is to draw a picture, and Willy's sure he can do it. Unfortunately, he spends too much time going on make-believe adventures. He never seems to complete his assignments.

Stevens, Kathleen, il. by Ray Bowler. **THE BEAST IN THE BATHTUB** (Harper & Row, 1985).

Lewis takes a bath with a huge, green beast. Later, they play together and have a pillow fight. Lewis's parents come looking for the beast, but they can't find him. (He's hiding under the bed!)

Stevenson, James. **ROLLING ROSE** (Greenwillow, 1992).

Baby Rose begins her adventures in her walker as she rolls out the back door and into the neighborhood. She gathers up a group of infants, all in their walkers. Rolling Rose and her 85 friends roll into the meadows and cornfields but are driven home by a rainstorm. At home, Rolling Rose is hugged, bathed, fed, and put to bed.

Stone, Kazuko G. **ALIGAY SAVES THE STARS** (Scholastic, 1991).

Aligay alligator throws his new boomerang so high it doesn't come back. The boomerang makes the stars and moon dizzy, so Aligay goes into space to retrieve his toy. However, he falls into the Milky Way. Luckily, all ends well when some stars return Aligay to Earth. Aligay uses his slingshot to send the stars back into the sky.

Strauss, Gwen, il. by Anthony Browne. **THE NIGHT SHIMMY** (Knopf, 1991).

Eric doesn't have to talk because he has an imaginary friend, Night Shimmy, who says everything for him. When Eric finds a real friend he wants to play with, he's not sure if he wants to give up his fantastic adventures.

Teague, Mark. **THE FIELD BEYOND THE OUTFIELD** (Scholastic, 1992).

While playing baseball, a young boy's imagination transforms the outfield into a towering stadium where fans watch two teams of human-sized insects play ball. The boy is whisked into the lineup, and his imagination allows him to overcome his jitters and hit in the winning run.

Tompert, Ann, il. by John Wallner. **LITTLE FOX GOES TO THE END OF THE WORLD** (Crown, 1976).

Little Fox explains to his mother what he'll do to get to the end of the world. Along the way, he'll capture the wind to sail to the island of giant one-eyed cats where he'll encounter tigers, bears, and monkeys. Then he'll have the North Wind bring him back home.

Townson, Hazel, il. by Mary Rees. **WHAT ON EARTH. . . ?** (Little, Brown, 1990).

Laura uses ordinary objects to pretend she's doing something wild and fantastic. While jumping on a chair, she imagines that it's a trampoline in a circus. While playing with the garden hose, she imagines she's on a high ladder putting out a fire. When she puts on her mother's winter coat, she imagines that she's a polar bear.

Turkle, Brinton. **DO NOT OPEN** (Dutton, 1981).

Miss Molly collects treasures that are left on the beach after a storm. She collects a banjo clock that doesn't work and some colored bottles. One day she finds a purple bottle labelled "DO NOT OPEN." When she opens it, a monster appears. Molly tricks the monster, and her wish comes true—her banjo clock begins to work.

Widman, Christine, il. by Lisa Desimini. **HOUSEKEEPER OF THE WIND** (Harper & Row, 1990).

Yula keeps house for the wind. She sweeps away autumn leaves, collects lost kites, and gathers the summer fragrances. However, one day Yula and the wind become angry with each other. Afterwards, both are sorry and apologize by giving each other special gifts.

Willard, Nancy, il. by Leo Diane and Lee Dillon. **PISH, POSH, SAID HIERONYMUS BOSCH** (Harcourt Brace, 1991).

In this imaginative poem, an artist named H. B. lives with many odd creatures such as the pickle-winged fish, three-legged thistles, a pigeon-toad rat, and a two-headed bat. The housekeeper tires of caring for these creatures and leaves, but later returns when the chores are shared by everyone.

Willis, Val, il. by John Shelley. **THE MYSTERY IN THE BOTTLE** (Farrar, Straus & Giroux, 1991).

Bobby Bell finds a bottle on the beach that contains a mermaid. His parents ignore his discovery until a crisis at the school swimming contest develops and Bobby and the mermaid come to the rescue.

Wood, Audrey, il. by Don Wood. **KING BIDGOOD'S IN THE BATHTUB** (Harcourt Brace, 1985).

The unruly King Bidgood refuses to leave his bathtub. The knight, queen, duke, and all the king's court attempt to persuade King Bidgood to leave his bath, but all fail. The problem is solved by a little page boy.

AS I WAS GOING OUT ONE DAY

As I was going out one day,
My head fell off and rolled away.
But when I saw that it was gone,
I picked it up and put it on.
And when I went into the street,
A fellow cried, "Look at your feet!"
I looked at them and sadly said,
"I've left them both asleep in bed!"
—Mother Goose

SEE, SEE!

See, see!
What shall I see?
A horse's head
Where his tail should be.
—Mother Goose

MOSES SUPPOSES HIS TOESES ARE ROSES

Moses supposes his toeses are roses,
But Moses supposes erroneously,
For nobody's toeses are posies of roses
As Moses supposes his toeses to be.
—Mother Goose

FLYING-MAN

Flying-man, Flying-man,
Up in the sky.
Where are you going to,
Flying so high?
Over the mountains
And over the sea,
Flying-man, Flying-man,
Can't you take me?
—Mother Goose

THERE WAS A YOUNG FARMER OF LEEDS

There was a young farmer of Leeds,
Who swallowed six packets of seeds.
It soon came to pass
He was covered with grass,
And he couldn't set down for the
    weeds!
—Mother Goose

ALAS! ALAS!

Alas! Alas! for Miss Mackay!
Her knives and forks have run away;
And when the cups and spoons are
    going,
She's sure there is no way of knowing.
—Mother Goose

NICHOLAS NED

Nicholas Ned,
He lost his head,
And put a turnip on instead;
But then, ah me!
He could not see,
So he thought it was night, and he went
    to bed.
—Author Unknown

IF ALL THE WORLD WERE APPLE PIE

If all the world were apple pie,
And all the seas were ink,
And all the trees were bread and
    cheese,
What should we have to drink?
—Anonymous

Make-Believe Songs and Action Verses

IF YOU'RE HAPPY

If you're happy and you know it,
Clap your hands. (clap, clap)
If you're happy and you know it,
Clap your hands. (clap, clap)
If you're happy and you know it,
Then your face will surely show it.
If you're happy and you know it,
Clap your hands. (clap, clap)
—Author Unknown

Other verses: angry (stomp your feet),
sad (cry a tear), silly (laugh a lot), sleepy
(go to sleep), happy (dance around).

I'M A LITTLE TEAPOT

I'm a little teapot,
Short and stout, (squat)
Here is my handle, (hand on hip)
Here is my spout. (bend elbow at waist)
When I get all steamed up,
Then I shout,
"Tip me over (bend in direction of bent
    elbow)
And pour me out."
—Author Unknown

Make up other verses pretending to be
different kinds of animals.

MAMA'S KNIVES AND FORKS

Here are Mama's knives and forks.
(Interlock fingers, palms up.)
This is Papa's table. (Turn palms down
    keeping fingers interlocked.)
Here is sister's little house. (Make peak
    with forefingers.)
This is baby's cradle. (Make peak with
    little fingers.)

MY BROTHER PLAYS THE VIOLIN

(Suit actions to each musical instrument.
Everyone repeats the last line.)

My brother plays the violin,
My sister plays the flute,
I love to play the trombone,
Root a toot, toot!

BEND AND STRETCH
(Suit actions to words.)

Bend and stretch, touch the stars.
I see Jupiter, there goes Mars.
Bend and stretch, touch the ground.
Oh, it's China I have found!

MAKE-BELIEVE ANIMALS
(Suit actions to words.)

I'm a rabbit, hop, hop, hop.
I'm a frog. I jump, jump, jump.
I'm a horsey, clop, clop, clop.
I'm a camel, here's my hump!
I'm a duck. I waddle, waddle.
I'm a birdie in a tree.
Off to school now, I won't dawdle.
I'm so happy being me.

I'M AN AIRPLANE

I'm an airplane with great big wings.
(Stretch out arms.)
My propeller spins around and sings,
Hummmmmmmmmmmmmmm! (Move
    one arm around.)
I go up. (Lift arms.)
I go down. (Lower arms.)
I fly high into the sky
Over my small town. (Turn around.)

More Make-believe Songs

"My Hand on My Head," p. 23, "Risseldy,
Rosseldy," p. 26, "Boom, Boom, Ain't It
Great to be Crazy," p. 30, "There's a Hole
in the Middle of the Sea," p. 50, and
"Down by the Bay," p. 57, in WEE SING
SILLY SONGS by Pamela Conn Beale and
Susan Hagen Nipp (Price/Stern/Sloan,
1985).

Make-Believe Games & Dramatic Play

SALLY GO 'ROUND THE SUN

Children join hands to form a circle and walk around while repeating the first verse as if circling the sun, moon, and chimney top. On "Yeah!" tell them to thrust their hands toward the middle of the circle and then back out. Have them continue the same actions when singing the second verse. Encourage the children to create other verses.

Sally go 'round the sun.
Sally go 'round the moon.
Sally go 'round the chimney top.
All in an afternoon. Yeah!
Sally go 'round the world.
Sally go 'round the room.
Sally go 'round the rocket ship.
All in an afternoon. Yeah!

THE DANCING SKELETON

This dramatization could be a full-scale production or done very simply without any props or costumes. If using props, you'll need the following items: recorded music, rocking chair, bench, fiddle, skeleton costume, and three actors to play a skeleton, widow, and fiddler. A purchased skeleton costume may be used, or create one by taping adhesive tape onto a black leotard. The child may use white makeup with black lines on the face or wear a skeleton mask. Record spooky music to use for the skeleton's entrance from the grave and fiddle music for the skeleton's dance. The widow may dress in black and narrate as the story is recreated. The fiddler wears a suit and pretends to play a fiddle while the recorded music plays. Show the children the book, and encourage them to make their own production. Older children will be able to perform the dramatization with little assistance or suggestions.

PANTOMIMES

A leader pretends to be doing something and the rest of the children must guess what the action is. Some action suggestions: drink something that is hot or cold or that tastes good or bad, make believe you're sewing and prick your finger, make believe you're sleepy—but trying to stay awake, or make believe that a bee is hovering above you trying to sting you.

MARBLES

After reading THE ADVENTURES OF ISABEL, or any time, let the children play marbles. Following is a reminder of how the game is played. Each player needs a designated number of colored marbles and a shooter marble. Use chalk to draw a circle on a smooth surface. Each child puts his or her marbles inside the circle and takes turns shooting at them with the shooter marble, using the thumb to thump the marble. The object is to see how many marbles can be knocked outside the circle. The player gets to keep all the marbles that roll outside the circle. At the end of the game, the marbles can be divided up evenly and another game played.

THE DANCING SKELETON

Materials: skeleton patterns, white paper, black marker or crayon, 9 brass fasteners, string, scissors

Directions: Have the children copy the skeleton patterns onto white paper, cut them out, and attach the pieces as indicated with brass fasteners. Help them attach a string to the skeleton's head to hold while making it dance.

FROG ON A LILY PAD

Materials: lily pad and frog patterns, green and white paper, wiggly eyes (optional), black and green markers or crayons, stapler, string, tissue paper, scissors, glue

Directions: Have each child cut out a lily pad from green paper using the pattern as a guide, and then attach four strings to hang it from the ceiling. Have the children cut out green paper frogs with white paper eyes (or use wiggly eyes). Have them draw other features using black for the pupils and dark green for spots. Help them attach the frog's back to the front by stapling part way around, then stuff tissue paper between the layers and continue to staple the rest of the way around. This will produce a frog with a fat tummy. Place the frog on its lily pad. Read TUESDAY in conjunction with this activity.

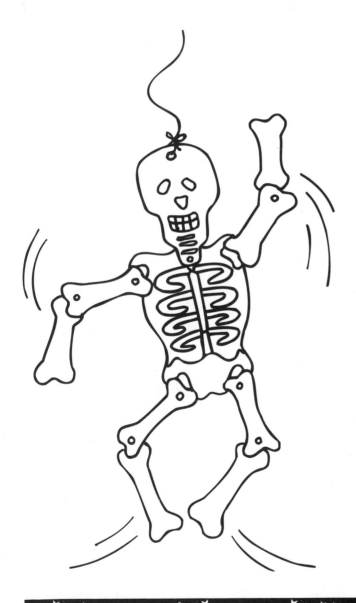

IMOGENE'S ANTLERS

Materials: antler pattern, brown paper, stapler, scissors

Directions: Have each child cut a 1 1/2" by 25" headband and a set of antlers from brown paper. Staple the antlers onto the headband, overlap the ends, and staple together to fit the child's head. After reading IMOGENE'S ANTLERS, the children will be inspired to make other headbands, too.

MOVEABLE ISABEL

Materials: poster paper, colored markers or chalk, scissors, brass brads

Directions: Use the opaque projector to enlarge an illustration of Isabel onto poster paper. Color and cut out. Cut off the arms and legs and reattach with brass brads. This gives Isabel the flexibility she needs to perform her mighty deeds. The children will enjoy manipulating Isabel in a variety of different positions.

MESS FAIRY

Materials: pink and purple paper, stick, glue, scissors, paper cup, tape, green pipe cleaners, pink paint, black paint, stick or yardstick

Directions: Use the illustration in the book to make a life-size Mess Fairy from pink paper. Add a three-dimensional nose by painting a paper cup pink, drawing on pig features, and taping to the Mess Fairy's face. Attach purple wings (see Magic Crafts in the Marvelous Magic chapter) and pipe cleaner antennae. Attach to a stick (yardsticks work well). The children may want to make their own smaller Mess Fairies to use when creating their own stories or retelling Fritz's tale.

Skeleton Pattern

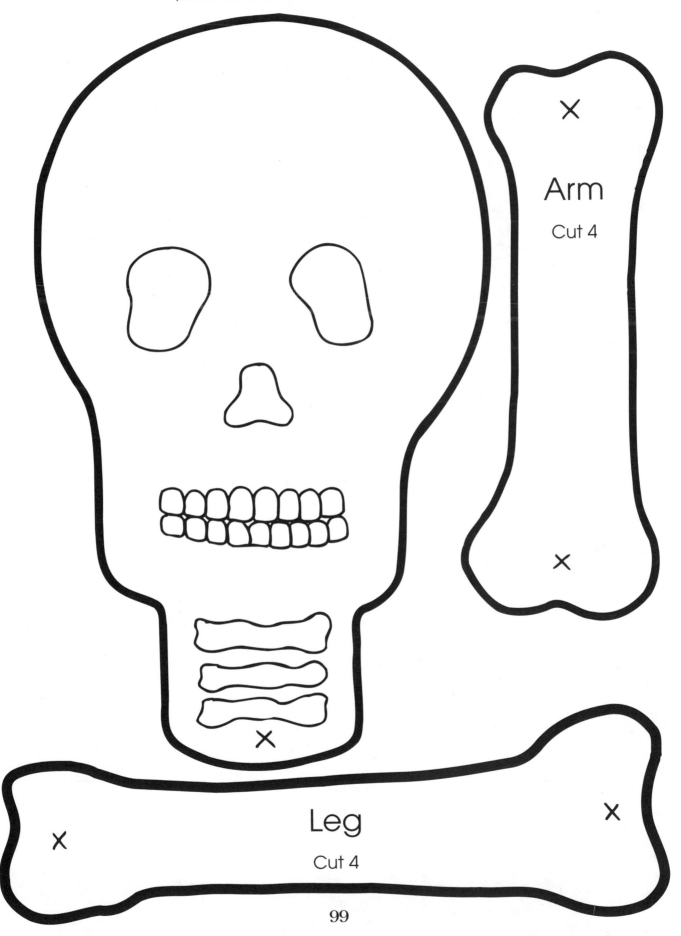

Arm

Cut 4

Leg

Cut 4

99

Skeleton Pattern

X X X X X X

Body

Cut 1

Frog Pattern

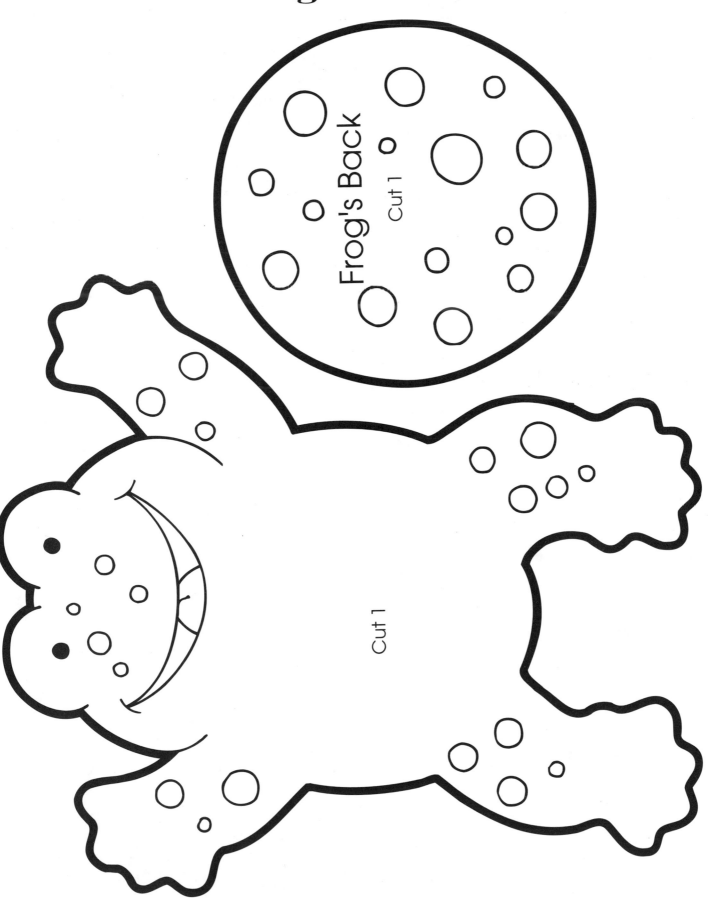

Frog's Back
Cut 1

Cut 1

Lily Pad Pattern

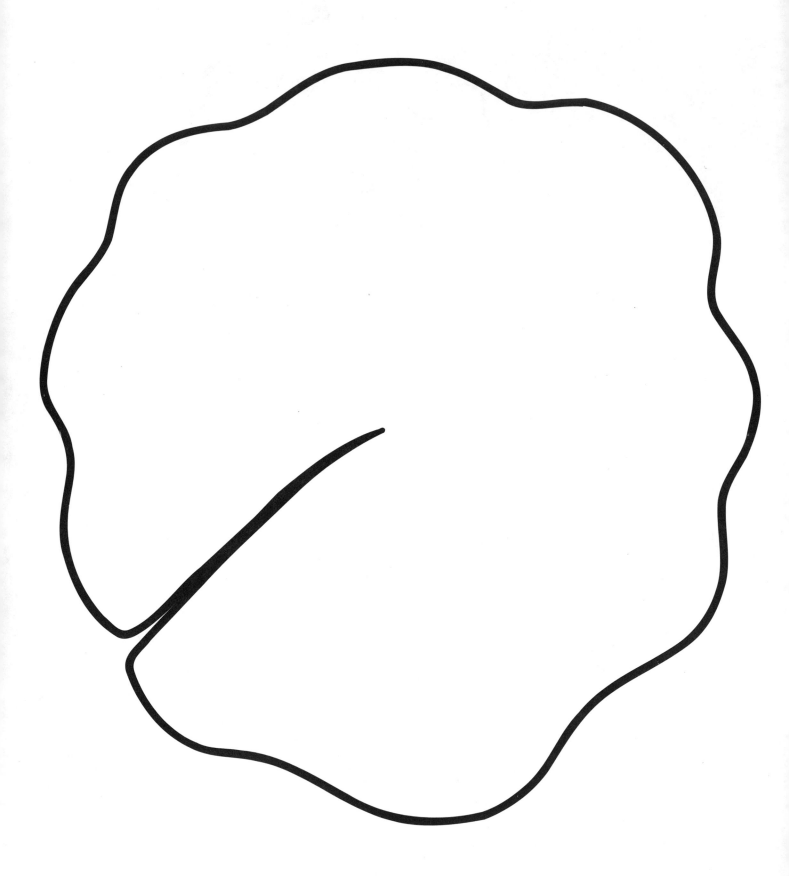

Antler Pattern

MAKE-BELIEVE FLYING SAUCERS
(makes about 4 dozen)

The colorful gumdrops give the effect of colored, flickering lights.

Blend together in a mixing bowl:
3/4 cup shortening
1/2 teaspoon salt
1 teaspoon grated lemon rind
1 1/2 cup sugar

Beat in:
1 egg
1/4 cup milk

Stir in:
3 cups flour
1 1/2 teaspoons baking powder
1 teaspoon soda
2 cups sliced gumdrops

Drop teaspoonfuls of the batter on lightly greased baking sheets. Grease the bottom of a glass, dip it in sugar, and flatten each saucer cookie slightly. Bake 8 to 10 minutes at 400 degrees. This snack is especially fun when served after reading IT CAME FROM OUTER SPACE.

BANANA MAN
(makes one serving)

1/2 banana
1 pineapple slice
raisins
cinnamon candy

Shave one side of the banana half slightly to make it lie flat. Cut the pineapple slice and adjust to fit around the banana to make a hat. Add raisins for eyes and a nose and cinnamon candy for the mouth. Place on a plate of shredded lettuce if desired. Children can make this nutritious snack themselves.

THREE MEN IN A TUB

Rub-a-dub-dub
Three men in a tub,
And who do you think they be?
The butcher, the baker and the
    candlestick maker;
Turn 'em out, knaves all three!
—Mother Goose

Recipe (makes one serving):
1/2 apple
cheese slice
3 cherries
toothpick

Scoop out the seeds from the apple half so that it looks like a boat. Cut a triangle sail from the cheese, insert the toothpick, and stand upright in the boat. Add 3 cherries on the edge of the boat and imagine that they're the butcher, the baker, and the candlestick maker.

FRITZ'S BRAN MUFFINS
(makes 20-24 muffins)

Stir together:
2 cups flour
1/2 cup sugar
5 teaspoons baking powder
1 1/2 teaspoons salt

Combine and add to flour mixture, stirring just until moistened:
2 beaten eggs
1 1/2 cups milk
2/3 cup cooking oil
2 cups bran flakes

Grease muffin tins or line with paper cups. Fill 2/3 full. Bake at 400 degrees for 20 to 25 minutes or until golden brown. Serve these muffins with lemonade.

Dreams can come true when you wish upon a star. But they can also come true when you wish upon a book: books allow readers to fly over cities, visit the ocean bottom, turn into an animal, live in a castle, or have a good friend. Anything can happen in a book.

After reading a few stories with the children, bring out a "Wish Bag" filled with books about wishing. When the children wish for a new book, give them one from the bag to enjoy. Then do several of the activities in this chapter concerning whimsical wishes.

Discuss with the children several of the traditional items that can be wished upon: a star, the new moon, a wishbone, a ladybug, a dandelion gone to seed, and birthday candles. Children will enjoy the Japanese custom of writing wishes on long paper streamers (you can use calculator tape) and tying them to tree branches.

To begin a story hour, wish that all the children sit quietly and listen intently!

SETTING THE STAGE

Make and attach red paper or cloth wings to a stuffed white rabbit to make Little Rabbit, the character in THE LITTLE RABBIT WHO WANTED RED WINGS by Carolyn Sherwin Bailey. Dress him in a pair of blue overalls to make him look even more authentic. Place Little Rabbit beside the book in a special corner to interest children in reading the story.

Make and hang a big yellow star in the corner of the room with the following poem printed on it:

Star light, star bright,
First star I see tonight.
I wish I may, I wish I might
Have the wish I wish tonight.

In the reading corner, put up a sign saying, "I wish you would read these books!" Place several books near the sign and change them often.

Fill a tub with water and place it on the floor for a wishing pond. Have a few pennies available for the children to toss into the pond while making a wish.

BULLETIN BOARD IDEAS

1. Enlarge and copy the provided illustration "I Wish Frogs Could Turn into Books!" Decorate with paint, crayons, or colored markers. Cut along the dotted lines and fold back as if opening a door. On the reverse side, print the title of a book about wishes. The idea is to show that when you make a wish the frogs turn into books!

2. Use an opaque projector to enlarge the cover of THE LITTLE RABBIT WHO WANTED RED WINGS. Make two separate red wings and attach to the art with brads so the wings will move. Pin up at an appropriate height to permit the children to move Little Rabbit's wings.

3. Enlarge a drawing of Fred Butterspoon from ONE BIG WISH and pin it up. Then pin up play money all over the board, making sure to partially cover Fred Butterspoon. Title the bulletin board "One Big Wish."

4. Title a bulletin board "When You Wish Upon a Book, Your Dreams Come True." Photocopy several book covers, or use real book covers if available, to pin up under the heading.

I Wish Frogs Could Turn Into Books!

AMANDA AND THE WITCH SWITCH
by John Himmelman (Puffin, 1987).

Story: Amanda is a friendly witch who wishes for only nice things. When she grants a toad three wishes, the toad uses his first wish to turn into a witch; then he turns Amanda into a toad. But don't worry about Amanda. At the end of the story, everything is changed back to normal.

Materials: an illustration of Amanda and her wand, scissors, a pebble, tape, marshmallows

Directions: Copy and enlarge an illustration of Amanda and her wand. Color and cut out, separating the wand and Amanda. Introduce the story by showing the children the moon wand. Talk about the wand and discuss who might own it. Introduce Amanda, tape on the wand, and read the story. At the conclusion, ask if any of the children would like to make a wish come true. Have a pebble and a marshmallow in your pocket. Show the pebble to the children and ask them to wish that the pebble would turn into a marshmallow. Put the pebble back into your pocket and bring out the marshmallow. Serve marshmallows to everyone. Then have the children make their own wands (see Wish Crafts.)

BARNEY BIPPLE'S MAGIC DANDELIONS
by Carol Chapman, il. by Steven Kellogg (E. P. Dutton, 1977).

Story: Miss Minerva Merkle gives Barney Bipple three magic dandelions as a reward for a good deed. She warns him not to wish for anything too complicated, but Barney doesn't heed the warning and his funny wishes get him into trouble.

Materials: dandelions gone to seed

Directions: Read this story when dandelions are in "bloom." Take the children to an open field where dandelions are growing. Have each child pick a dandelion, make a wish, and blow the seeds into the air. If it's not possible to go on a field trip, very carefully bring dandelions into the classroom and let the children make wishes there. Note: Be careful not to spread seeds where they will be unwelcome. Dandelions multiply rapidly.

IF WE COULD MAKE WISHES

by Adelaide Holl, il. by Judy Pelikan
(Garrard, 1977).

Story: A young boy and girl imagine all
the wonderful things they would do if
their wishes came true. They would have
a pet fire-breathing dragon and a
dinosaur to ride. They would turn the
world upside down and have a polka
dot sky.

Materials: pop-up wish cups (see Wish
Crafts)

Directions: After reading the story, the
children will want to think about all of
the things they could do if their own
wishes came true. Bring out the wish
cups. Ask the children to wish with you
for one of the illustrations you put in the
wish cups, for example, a candy tree.
Because it's a wish cup, the wish will
come true—just push the candy tree up
out of the cup. Do this with other wishes.
The children will want to make their own
wish cup with their very own wish inside.

THE LITTLE RABBIT WHO WANTED RED WINGS

by Carolyn Sherwin Bailey, il. by Chris
Santoro (Platt & Munk, 1978).

Story: Little Rabbit wishes for a bushy tail
like Gray Squirrel's or a back full of
bristles like Mr. Porcupine's. His wish
comes true when he asks for a pair of
red wings, but no one recognizes him so
he decides it's best to be himself.

Materials: rabbit with wings (see Wish
Crafts), tub of water

Directions: After reading the story,
encourage each child to make his or
her own Little Rabbit. Attach strings and
hang the rabbits from the ceiling as if
they're flying. Set out the "wishing
pond" for the children to look into while
making a wish. Don't forget to explain
that the wishing is all in fun. Refer to
Setting the Stage and Bulletin Board
Ideas for additional activities.

ONE BIG WISH
by Jay Williams, il. by John O'Brien
(Macmillan, 1980).

Story: When farmer Fred Butterspoon cuts away the brambles from an old woman's dress, she grants him one wish. He wishes for all of his wishes to come true. After a series of foolish wishes, the farmer decides that the only wish he really wants is to wish the old woman a good morning.

Materials: play money

Directions: Encourage the children to dramatize this story using play money, or money they make from green paper. Assist them in acting out the story at first, then have them do it by themselves. The children can also create a new story line and change the wishes.

THREE WISHES
by Lucille Clifton, il. by Michael Hayes
(Doubleday, 1992).

Story: Nobie finds a good luck penny on New Year's Day with her birth year on it. Now she can make three wishes. She's surprised when her first two wishes do come true, and uses her third wish to wish for friendship—her most valued possession.

Materials: pennies

Directions: Hide pennies throughout the room so that every child can find one with his or her birth year on it. If a child finds one with the wrong year, he or she should put it back for someone else to find. Let the children keep their penny and make three wishes on it.

THE THREE WISHES

retold by M. Jean Crain, il. by Yuri Salzman (Scholastic, 1968).

Story: In this classic tale, a tree fairy grants a woodcutter three wishes. He and his wife plan to wish for a castle, a carriage, and lots of jewels. However, through their foolishness, they waste all three wishes: the woodcutter wishes for a sausage, wishes it on the end of his wife's nose, and then must use his third wish to get it off again. (But they do have sausage for dinner that night.)

Materials: pantyhose, string, elastic, safety pin, materials for paper sausage (see Wish Crafts)

Directions: Ahead of time, make a sausage from pantyhose by stuffing the toe with scraps of the pantyhose and tying it on the ends to look like a sausage. Safety pin the sausage to a piece of elastic that fits comfortably around your head. After reading the story, turn your back to the children and slip on the sausage, making it appear to be "attached" to your nose. Be prepared for lots of laughs! Complain that you don't like the sausage on the end of your nose, and ask the children to wish it off. Then let the children make their own sausages.

In a version of this story retold by Margot Zemach (Farrar, Straus & Giroux, 1986), a string of sausages becomes attached to the woodcutter's nose. The children will delight in seeing the differences in the two stories.

THE WISHING HAT

by Annegert Fuchshuber (Morrow, 1977).

Story: In this lighthearted tale from Germany, a free-spirited man finds a wishing hat that grants his wishes: an apple tree in the living room, a basket that goes shopping by itself, and an umbrella that flies him over the city. People call the man a simpleton for not wishing for cars or houses, but he enjoys his own way of life.

Materials: straw hat decorated like the one in the story, red apples

Directions: Explain that your wishing hat grants wishes. Put it on, close your eyes, turn the hat around three times, and wish that there were a story about a hat. Produce THE WISHING HAT book as if it appeared magically and read it, showing the delightful illustrations. Then let the children use the hat to make their own wishes, explaining first that everything is make believe. Serve red apples that you tell the children came from the tree in the old man's living room.

Bently, Nancy, il. by Don Madden. **I'VE GOT YOUR NOSE** (Doubleday, 1991).

Nahzella the witch turns into a fairy god-mother and sets forth to find a scarier nose. She wishes she had the baker's big red nose for herself and that the baker had the farmer's. Then she wishes for the butcher's nose, but gets a basset hound's instead. Finally she wishes all noses back to their rightful owner and decides that's the best after all.

Bush, John, il. by Karky Paul. **THE FISH WHO COULD WISH** (Scholastic, 1991).

This story is told in rhyme. A fish who lives in the deep blue sea wishes for a castle, a car, a horse, snow, and to fly around the world. All his wishes come true, but one day he wishes he could be like all the other fish, and that is his very last wish.

Chess, Victoria. **POOR ESME** (Holiday House, 1982).

Everyone is too busy to play with Esme, so she checks out a library book on how to make wishes come true. Unfortun-ately, that doesn't work either, but her wish is finally granted when her mother brings home a new baby for Esme to play with.

Collins, David R., il. by David Wiesner. **THE ONE BAD THING ABOUT BIRTHDAYS** (Harcourt Brace, 1981).

David can't decide what to wish for as he blows out the candles on his birthday cake. He'd like an endless amount of Grandma's cookies, a fishing trip with Grandpa, or a later bedtime so that he can watch a scary monster movie. He finally decides to wish that he didn't have to wait a whole year to make another birthday wish.

Damjan, Mischa, il. by Hans de Beer. **THE BIG SQUIRREL AND THE RHINOCEROS** (North-South, 1990).

In the land of a Thousand Shadows, the little animals are unhappy because they think that the big animals are taking advantage of them. One night they wish to change places with the big animals, and in the morning their wish has come true. However, everyone soon decides that it's best to have both sets of animals back to their normal size.

Gag, Wanda. **MILLIONS OF CATS** (Cow-ard, McCann & Geoghegan, 1977).

A lonely old woman wishes for a sweet little fluffy cat to keep her company. Her husband goes to get one but when he can't decide which one to take, he brings home millions of cats. The cats get into a terrible quarrel and eat each other. Only one scraggly cat remains, who makes the couple a fine pet.

Haas, Irene. **THE MAGGIE B.** (Aladdin, 1975).

A little girl named Margaret Barnstable wishes for a boat named after her that she could sail for a day. She also wishes for someone nice to accompany her. The little girl's wishes come true—the boat is called "The Maggie B." and her sweet brother James goes with her on their imaginary sailing trip.

Howe, James, il. by Ed Young. **I WISH I WERE A BUTTERFLY** (Gulliver, 1987).

A despondent cricket refuses to make music because he's ugly (that's what the frog at the edge of the pond told him). The cricket wishes he could be a beautiful butterfly, but of course his wish cannot come true. Luckily, a wise spider helps the cricket realize that he's special in his own way.

Joose, Barbara M., il. by Emily Arnold McCully. **DINAH'S MAD, BAD WISHES** (Harper & Row, 1989).

Dinah and Mama become angry with each other and Dinah wishes Mama would grow a sausage nose and warts all over her face. Then Dinah gets scared when she thinks her wishes might come true, and the two forget their angry feelings and hug each other.

LeSieg, Theo. **PLEASE TRY TO REMEMBER THE FIRST OF OCTEMBER** (Random House, 1977).

In this lighthearted book, Octember the first is the day all outlandish wishes come true—even wishes for two green kangaroos, a pickle tree, or a new skateboard TV.

Lester, Helen, il. by Lynn Munsinger. **POOKINS GETS HER WAY** (Houghton Mifflin, 1987).

Little Pookins always gets her own way. She eats ice cream for breakfast and has all the toys she wants. One day she meets a gnome who grants her all her wishes and she soon learns there's more to happiness than having everything she wants.

Levine, Abby and Sarah, il. by Blanche Sims. **SOMETIMES I WISH I WERE MINDY** (Albert Whitman, 1986).

A girl wishes she were her friend Mindy, who is rich, has her own beautiful room and lots of toys, and can buy any clothes she wants. Although the little girl realizes she has everything she needs plus a loving family, she's still a little envious of Mindy.

Littledale, Freya, il. by Barbara Lovalle. **THE SNOW CHILD** (Scholastic, 1989).

In this Russian folk tale, a lonely man and woman wish for a child of their own. When they build a snow child, it becomes real and they all live together very happily. Spring comes and the snow child must leave, but every winter it returns to bring them joy.

Margolis, Richard J., il. by Robert Lopshire. **WISH AGAIN, BIG BEAR!** (Macmillan, 1972).

Big Bear catches a wish-fish who agrees to give the bear three wishes if he won't eat him. However, the wish-fish deceives the bear by telling him he's small and graceful when actually he's not. Luckily, the ruse turns out all right and the two become good friends.

Maris, Ron. **I WISH I COULD FLY** (Greenwillow, 1986).

Turtle wishes he could fly like a bird, dive like a frog, climb like a squirrel, and run like a rabbit. But when it rains and all the animals must run for cover, turtle decides it's not so bad to be a turtle after all. Also available as a Big Book.

Rylant, Cynthia, il. by Peter Catalanotto. **AN ANGEL FOR SOLOMAN SINGER** (Orchard, 1992).

A lonely New York City man, Soloman Singer, doesn't like living in the city in a hotel. He wishes he could have a porch, a fireplace, and a pet. However, he finds good cheer and companionship from a waiter named Angel at the Westway Cafe.

Sato, Satoru, il. by Tsutomu Murakami. **I WISH I HAD A BIG, BIG TREE** (Lothrop, Lee & Shepard, 1989).

Kaoru looks out the window into the yard and wishes he had a big tree. He imagines he would climb and hide in the tree and build a tree house where he would make pancakes for the squirrels and birds who would visit. When Kaoru discovers his father had the same wish when he was a boy, they plant a tree together.

Schweninger, Ann. **BIRTHDAY WISHES** (Viking Kestrel, 1986).

Buttercup, a rabbit, is planning all the festivities for her upcoming fifth birthday. There are invitations, balloons, birthday cake, and presents. Then Buttercup's birthday wishes come true—she has a wonderful birthday.

Sharmat, Marjorie Weinman, il. by Janet Stevens. **TWITCHELL, THE WISHFUL** (Holiday House, 1981).

Twitchell Mouse envies his friends' belongings: Claudette's warm fireplace, Jacqueline's new shoes, Granville's fine violin, Thackery's oak table, and Norman's exciting trips to Australia. After Twitchell gets everything he wants, he decides he's happiest with his own things.

Stevenson, James. **THE WISH CARD RAN OUT** (Greenwillow, 1981).

Charlie is exuberant when he finds a wish card from International Wish. However, the adventures begin when Charlie tries to undo a wish. Suddenly his dog can talk, the fairy godmother retires, the wish card expires, and a bunch of computers chase him.

Thurber, James, il. by Marc Simont. **MANY MOONS** (Harcourt Brace, 1990).

Princess Leonore's wish for the moon cannot be fulfilled by any of the wise men. Then a clever jester solves the problem by making her a tiny round golden moon strung on a golden chain.

Tobias, Tobi, il. by Trina Schart. **JANE, WISHING** (Viking, 1977).

Jane wishes for long red hair that she could wear loose every day. She also wishes that she were an only child, that she had her own room full of beautiful things, and that she could have a different name. But she knows all her wishes won't come true so she decides to be happy anyway.

Waber, Bernard. **YOU'RE A LITTLE KID WITH A BIG HEART** (Houghton Mifflin, 1980).

A magic kite grants a young girl, Octavia Blisswink, her wish to be a grown-up. However, Octavia soon discovers that being an adult is not so great and wishes she were a little girl once more. That wish won't come true until she finds the magic kite again.

Walter, Mildred Pitts, il. by Diane and Leo Dillon. **BROTHER TO THE WIND** (Lothrop, Lee & Shepard, 1985).

A young African boy wishes he could fly. His grandmother tells him about Good Snake, who makes wishes come true. After a long search the boy finds Good Snake, follows all his directions, and his wish to fly does come true.

Washington, Ned, il. by Alexandra Day. **WHEN YOU WISH UPON A STAR** (Green Tiger Press, 1987).

This favorite song is illustrated here in full color. The lyrics are made a part of the illustrations on each page, and they become better hidden as the book progresses. A record of the song accompanies this book.

Wish Poems, Songs, & Action Verses

MOTHER GOOSE RHYMES

Touch blue,
Your wish will come true.

What comes out of a chimney?
Smoke.
May your wish and my wish
Never be broke.

Star light, star bright,
First star I see tonight,
I wish I may, I wish I might,
Have the wish I wish tonight.

If wishes were horses,
Beggars would ride;
If turnips were watches,
I would wear one by my side.

A KITE

I often sit and wish that I
Could be a kite up in the sky,
And ride upon the breeze and go
Whichever way I chanced to blow.
—Anonymous

I WISH

(Suit actions to words.)

I wish I had a broom,
To ride around the room.
I wish I had a nickel,
To buy myself a pickle.
I wish I had a sister,
So I could kiss her.
I wish I had a book,
So I could look, look, look!

IF I HAD THREE WISHES

If I had three wishes,
That could come true,
(Hold up three fingers.)
I'd wish for a friend
Just like you.
(Point to friend.)
I'd wish for a bird
Colored blue.
(Flap arms.)
And I'd wish for a cow
That would moo.
(Moo.)

More Wish Poems and Songs

"I Wish That My Room Had a Floor," p. 34, in FOR LAUGHING OUT LOUD: POEMS TO TICKLE YOUR FUNNYBONE, selected by Jack Prelutsky, (Knopf, 1991).

"The Wish," p. 29 and "Wish," p. 26, in READ-ALOUD RHYMES FOR THE VERY YOUNG, selected by Jack Prelutsky, il. by Marc Brown (Knopf, 1986).

"Lester," p. 69, in WHERE THE SIDEWALK ENDS by Shel Silverstein (Harper & Row, 1974).

"I Wish I Were a Circus Clown," p. 47 and "Said This Little Fairy," p. 81, in RING A RING O'ROSES: FINGER PLAYS FOR PRE-SCHOOL CHILDREN (Flint Public Library, 1988).

TWINKLE, TWINKLE LITTLE STAR (A Lullaby Book with Lights and Music), il. by Jannat Messenger (Aladdin, 1986).

WHEN YOU WISH UPON A STAR by Ned Washington, il. by Alexander Day (Green Tiger Press, 1987).

I WISH I WERE AN ANIMAL

Each player decides which animal he or she wishes to be. Examples: cat, dog, sheep, goat, duck, lion, horse, or cow. More than one player may want to be the same animal.

The players stand in a circle. A designated player begins the game by standing on tiptoes. The next player to the right crouches and imitates his or her animal. Then the next player imitates his or her animal, and so on, with each child briefly performing.

For variety, the designated leader may command different animals to make their sounds and actions at different times, for example, calling out for the pigs, cows, and ducks to perform together. As a finale, have all animals perform together.

I WISH I COULD CATCH THE PAPER

Any number of children may play this game, but each must have a partner. One player stands on a chair and drops a thin sheet of paper. The other player wishes he or she could catch the paper as it falls to the floor. Players may use only their index fingers and thumbs to catch the falling paper. When a player's wish comes true (or after several tries), the partners change places.

GRANTING WISHES

Materials needed: pebble, marshmallow, toy frog, book, leaves, costume jewels, paper clips, coins, flowers, doll, pot or box

Put the marshmallow, book, jewels, coins, and doll into a magic pot or box. Lay the other objects out on a table. Designate one child to be the wish granter. He or she may wear a crown and have a wand. The wish granter asks another child to pick up one of the objects not in the pot, such as a flower, and then explains that if the child wishes to turn the object into a doll, he or she must put it into the magic pot and say, "I wish this (object) would turn into a doll." The wish granter then waves the wand over the pot and brings out the doll.

While the children know the objects aren't really changing, they love the pretending and want to play this simple game again and again. The game is especially meaningful after reading AMANDA AND THE WITCH SWITCH by John Himmelman.

WAND AND CROWN

Wand

Materials: star pattern, glue, scissors, sparkles, dowel stick, yellow paper

Directions: Use the pattern to cut out two stars from the yellow paper. Glue sparkles onto one side of each star. Glue the two plain sides together, and slip the two-sided star onto the stick before the glue dries. The result is a sparkling wand for granting wishes.

Crown

Materials: star pattern, yellow construction paper, stapler, scissors, sparkles, glue, ruler or tape measure

Directions: Cut a headband from the yellow paper that measures 2" X 23". Overlap and staple the ends together to fit the child's head. Use the pattern to cut out a star. Glue on sparkles if desired and staple onto the headband.

WISH CUPS

Materials: wish patterns, 10 oz. paper cups, scissors, plastic drinking straws, tape

Directions: Insert a straw through the bottom of a cup. Make two copies of a wish pattern or a wish design the children can make and tape them to the end of the straw so the illustrations are double-sided. Use the cups for making wishes come true. Wish for a candy tree and up one pops from the cup. The children love it! They will want to make several.

WISH CARDS

Materials: wish card pattern, copy paper

Directions: After reading THE WISH CARD RAN OUT by James Stevenson, make copies of the pattern for the children to use for making wishes.

STAND-UP CATS

Materials: cat pattern, variety of colored paper, scissors, crayons or markers

Directions: Use the cat pattern and follow the directions for making various different colored cats. The children should make as many as they like so there will appear to be a million cats. Set the cats on a shelf along with the book MILLIONS OF CATS.

RABBIT WITH WINGS

Materials: rabbit and wing patterns, white and red construction paper, scissors, brass brads, string

Directions: Use the patterns to cut out white rabbits and red wings. Help the children attach the wings with brads as illustrated. Hang from the ceiling as if the rabbits are flying. Do this activity in conjunction with the reading of THE LITTLE RABBIT WHO WANTED RED WINGS.

PAPER SAUSAGE

Materials: sausage pattern, scissors, tape, brown construction paper

Directions: Use the pattern to cut out sausages from brown construction paper. Then let the children tape the sausages to their noses to dramatize the Three Wishes story or to create their own version.

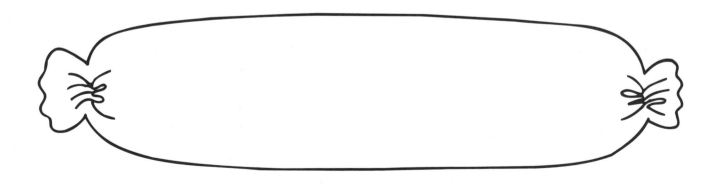

Wish Patterns

Cat Pattern

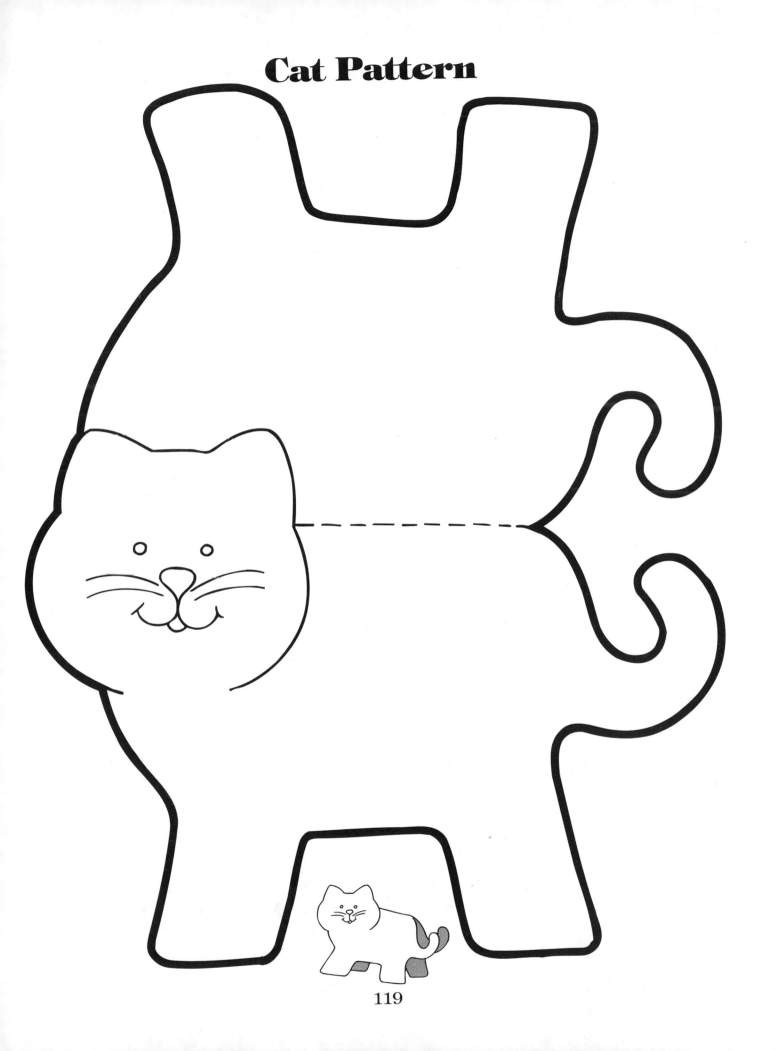

Rabbit and Wings Patterns

Star and Wish Card Patterns

Wish Snacks

THREE WISHES POPCORN SNACK

Wish for popcorn, peanuts, and raisins and you'll get a new taste treat.

Mix together:
1 qt. popped popcorn
1/2 cup unsalted peanuts
1/2 cup raisins

Melt in saucepan:
2 tablespoons peanut butter

Pour peanut butter over popcorn mixture and toss to coat.

WISHING STARS

Place three cups of water in a saucepan. Sprinkle 6 envelopes of unflavored gelatin over the water. Cook until gel-atin is dissolved (it should come to a boil).

Stir in one 12-ounce can of frozen orange juice and stir until the juice is melted.

Pour into a 9" X 13" baking pan and chill until set. Use a star cookie cutter (or the star pattern provided in the Wish Crafts section) to cut out stars. Enjoy eating the scraps also!

Wishing stars may also be made from a rolled sugar cookie recipe and frosted with yellow or white frosting. Add candied sparkles if desired.

WISHING HATS

Place a mini scoop of ice cream, an ice cream bonbon, or a marshmallow on a cookie or graham cracker to make a delicious hat.

BIRTHDAY CUPCAKES

Make cupcakes for everyone. Frost and insert a candle in each. Sing "Happy Birthday" to each other and have all of the children make a wish and blow out the candles. Read THE ONE BAD THING ABOUT BIRTHDAYS or BIRTHDAY WISHES.

MILLIONS OF CATS

Make your favorite rolled sugar cookie recipe. Cut out shapes with cat cookie cutter or the cat pattern below. Decorate with frosting. Be sure to read MILLIONS OF CATS!

RESOURCES

BOOKS

Bauer, Caroline Feller. **CELEBRATIONS** (H.W. Wilson, 1985).

Bauer, Caroline Feller. **HANDBOOK FOR STORYTELLERS** (American Library Assoc., 1977).

Bauer, Caroline Feller. **THIS WAY TO BOOKS** (H.W. Wilson, 1983).

Beall, Pamela Conn and Susan Hagen Nipp. **WEE SING** (Price/Stern/Sloan, 1982).

Beall, Pamela Conn and Susan Hagen Nipp. **WEE SING AND PLAY** (Price/Stern/Sloan, 1985).

Beall, Pamela Conn and Susan Hagen Nipp. **WEE SING SILLY SONGS** (Price/Stern/Sloan, 1983).

Catron, Carol Elaine and Barbara Catron Parks. **SUPER STORY TELLING** (T.S. Denison, 1986).

Courson, Diane, il. by Elizabeth Nygaard. **LET'S LEARN ABOUT FAIRY TALES AND NURSERY RHYMES** (Good Apple, 1988).

de Paola, Tomie. **TOMIE DE PAOLA'S MOTHER GOOSE** (Putnam, 1985).

Dowell, Ruth I., il. by Concetta C. Scott. **MOVE OVER, MOTHER GOOSE** (Gryphon House, 1987).

Evans, Joy and Jo Ellen Moore. **FUN WITH BOOKS** (Evan-Moor, 1987).

Evans, Joy and Jo Ellen Moore. **MORE FUN WITH BOOKS** (Evan-Moor, 1987).

Flint Public Library. **RING A RING O'ROSES: FINGER PLAYS FOR PRE-SCHOOL CHILDREN** (Flint Public Library, 1026 E. Kearsley St., Flint, MI 48502, 1988).

Glazer, Tom. **EYE WINKER, TOM TINKER, CHIN CHOPPER** (Doubleday, 1973).

Hearne, Betsy. **CHOOSING BOOKS FOR CHILDREN** (Delacorte, 1981).

Kimmel, Margaret Mary and Elizabeth Segel. **FOR READING OUT LOUD!** (Dell, 1983).

Landsberg, Michelle. **READING FOR THE LOVE OF IT** (Prentice-Hall, 1987).

Lima, Caroyln W. and John A. **A TO ZOO SUBJECT ACCESS TO CHILDREN'S PICTURE BOOKS** (R.R. Bowker, 1989).

Maquire, Jack. **CREATIVE STORYTELLING** (McGraw-Hill, 1985).

Oppenheim, Joanne, Barbara Brenner and Betty D. Boegehold. **CHOOSING BOOKS FOR KIDS** (Ballantine, 1986).

POEMS TO READ TO THE VERY YOUNG selected by Josette Frank, il. by Eloise Wilkin. (Random House, 1982).

Prelutsky, Jack, il. by James Stevenson. **THE NEW KID ON THE BLOCK** (Greenwillow, 1984).

Prelutsky, Jack, il. by Garth Williams. **RIDE A PURPLE PELICAN** (Greenwillow 1986).

THE RANDOM HOUSE BOOK OF POETRY FOR CHILDREN selected by Jack Prelutsky, il. by Marc Brown (Random House, 1983).

READ-ALOUD RHYMES FOR THE VERY YOUNG selected by Jack Prelutsky, il. by Marc Brown (Knopf, 1986).

Riggrers, Maxine. **AMAZING ALLIGATORS** (Monday Morning Books, 1990).

Silverstein, Shel. **A LIGHT IN THE ATTIC** (Harper & Row, 1981).

Silverstein, Shel. **WHERE THE SIDEWALK ENDS** (Harper & Row, 1974).

Sitarz, Paula Gaj. **PICTURE BOOK STORY HOURS** (Libraries Unlimited, 1987).

Trelease, Jim. **THE READ-ALOUD HAND-BOOK** (Penguin, 1982).

Wendelin, Karla Hawkins, and M. Jean Greenlaw. **STORYBOOK CLASSROOMS** (Humanics, 1986).

White, Mary Lou, editor. **ADVENTURING WITH BOOKS** (National Council of Teachers of English, 1981).

PROPS

A Child's Collection, 155 Avenue of the Americas, New York, NY 10013

Creative Teaching Press, P.O. Box 6017, Cypress, CA 90630-0017

Folkmanis, Inc., 1219 Park Avenue, Emeryville, CA 94608

Peaceable Kingdom Press, 2954 Hillegass Avenue, Berkeley, CA 94705

Trudy Toy Company, Norwalk, KY

METRIC CONVERSION CHART:

Temperatures:
To convert Fahrenheit to Celsius, subtract 32 and multiply by 5/9.

205 F = 96.1 C
300 F = 148.8 C
325 F = 162.8 C
350 F = 177 C (baking)
375 F = 190.5 C
400 F = 204.4 C (hot oven)
425 F = 218.3 C
450 F = 232 C (very hot oven)

Capacity:
1/2 teaspoon = 2.5 ml.
1 teaspoon = 5 ml.
5 teaspoons = 25 ml.
1 tablespoon = 15 ml.
1/4 cup = 59.25 ml.
1/3 cup = 79 ml.
1/2 cup = 118.5 ml.
2/3 cup = 158 ml.
3/4 cup = 177.75 ml.
1 cup = 237 ml.
1 1/2 cups = 355.5 ml.

Weight:
1 ounce = 28.3 grams
7 ounces = 198.1 grams

Length:
1/8 inch = .3175 cm.
1/4 inch = .635 cm.
1 inch = 2.54 cm.
1 foot = 30.48 cm.

INDEX